Death & The Caring Community

Death & The Caring Community

Ministering to the Terminally Ill

LARRY RICHARDS

PAUL JOHNSON, M.D.

MULTNOMAH PRESS
Portland, Oregon 97266

Cover design and illustration by Britt Taylor Collins.

DEATH AND THE CARING COMMUNITY
©1980 by Multnomah Press
Portland, Oregon

First printing, 1980
Printed in the United States of America

Library of Congress Cataloging in Publication Data

Richards, Lawrence O
    Death and the caring community.

    Bibliography: p. 195
    Includes indexes.
    1. Pastoral medicine. 2. Church work with the
    sick. 3. Terminal care—Moral and religious aspects.
I. Johnson, Paul, 1915-   joint author. II. Title.
BV 4335.R52   259'.4   80-19752
ISBN 0-930014-45-6

Contents

Chapter 1

Family, Gathered Around

*A*s Cathy's cancer grew worse, and the treatment more and more draining, she simply had to stay at the hospital. But her last months were far from lonely.

About four years before her illness, Cathy had become a Christian through a women's Bible study group started by a Young Life leader. When that group grew into a church the next year, Cathy was one of the original members of the Fellowship. Of course, Bob hadn't come, except to the dinner parties the members of the Fellowship gave. He and her grown children weren't Christians, and had no interest in the faith.

And then the cancer came.

Cathy died. But she didn't die alone. Day after day, for a period of months, brothers and sisters from her Fellowship drove the 35 miles from their mountain community to the Denver hospital. No one told them they should. No one organized shifts. But all during the days and the evenings, brothers and sisters who loved Cathy were with her. And when she had a particularly difficult time, there would be those who stayed through the night.

Back at home people gathered around Bob, too. The men took him out to lunch, and insisted he go with them to play tennis. One of the Fellowship family came over daily to feed the dog and care for Cathy's plants. Cathy, and Bob too, were surrounded by a supportive love that told each of them: you are significant. You are important to us, and to God.

When Cathy died over a dozen of her friends were there to see her off.

It had been a difficult time for Cathy. She'd known the same feelings and doubts and fears that others know as they pass through a terminal illness. But for Cathy there was something different than many others' experience. There was a surrounding warmth and love that flowed from a supportive community of those who cared.

The Caring Community

Today one of the most significant issues facing all Christians is to understand the nature of the Church. Many forces press the Church into institutional molds. Many advocate a spiritual leadership which is modeled on the latest management theories. But Scripture calls us back to rediscover our identity as it has been established and revealed by God.

Paul guides us toward a biblical understanding as he tells of one of his prayers. "I kneel before the Father," Paul reports, "from whom his whole family in heaven and on earth derives its name" (Ephesians 3:14). In Old and New Testament times every "name" was significant, being a revelation of the character or work of the person or thing named. In essence, a name was intended to communicate identity. Thus to say that we take our name from God is to affirm that we must come to understand who we are by the name-identity God gives us.

What then is our identity? First, Paul names God: "I kneel before the *Father*." In Himself, God sums up all the love and caring, the discipline and guidance, that fatherhood implies. And Paul teaches that it is from God, in His self-revelation as Father, that we derive our identity. He specifies our identity in the phrase "*his whole family* in heaven and on earth." Because God is Father, and we Christians share a common relationship to Him as His children, *we are family*.

The family emphasis is consistent throughout the New Testament. We see it over and over again in the address of Christians as brothers and sisters. We see it stated explicitly in many New Testament letters. "You are all sons of God through faith in Christ Jesus," Galatians tells us (3:26). "Both the one who makes men holy and those who are made holy are of the same family," Hebrews affirms (2:11), and goes on, "since the children have flesh and blood, he too shared in their humanity" (2:14). We are brothers and sisters in a Family of which God is Father, and Jesus is Son. On the basis of our shared relationship with the Father, we are urged to live together as children of God's household (Galatians 6:10; Ephesians 2:19).

Scripture describes the relationships that are to grow between members of the family. "My brothers," Paul exhorts the Galatians, "serve one another in love" (5:13). Peter says, "Now that you have purified yourselves by obeying the truth so that you have sincere love for your brothers, love one another deeply, from the heart (1 Peter 1:22). John encourages Christlike, self-sacrificial love in the family, and says, "we ought to lay down our lives for our brothers. If anyone has material possessions and sees his brother in need but has no pity on him, how can the love of God be in him? Dear children, let us not love with words or tongue but with actions and in truth" (1 John 3:16-18). With all these exhortations to *be* the family that we *are,* the Scriptures give abundant illustrations of hospitality, bearing one another's burdens, caring for the fatherless and oppressed, kindness, warmth, and that supportive love which makes the family of God a caring community.

As we go on in this book, it is this concept of the Church —not as an institution, but as a family of caring people— which provides the framework within which our response to those with life-threatening illnesses can be made. When we write of "church," or speak of "what the church can do," we will not be giving suggestions for organizing programs or for structuring agencies. Instead we will show how people who care for their hurting brothers and sisters can respond, lovingly and supportively, to people like Cathy and Bob. We will explore the Christian's response to very real needs, which are increasingly experienced in our modern society.

Very Real Needs

There have always been very real needs created for those with life-threatening illnesses and for their families. But changes in the pattern of life of our culture have tended to multiply both the frequency and severity of needs today. The support which can be provided by a caring Christian community has become even more vital.

One of the changes that makes caring for the terminally ill a special need today is represented in the following chart which shows the major causes of death in the United States in 1900 and 1972.

The charts sketch a striking picture. Comparing the deaths per 100,000 we immediately see that people tend to live much longer. Actually, in 1900, 53% of all deaths recorded in the United States were of children under the age of 15! In 1900 the average lifespan in industrial countries was 47. Today a Caucasian man in the United States can expect to live more than 72 years, and a woman 75. Death is increasingly reserved for the old; witnessing death is not a normal or common experience for the majority in our under-40 society.

Along with the increase in lifespan has come a change in the causes of death. Today most killing diseases are degenerative — diseases which not only strike the older among us, but which also tend to be lingering illnesses. The longer the process of dying, the greater the stress on both the individual and his or her family. Where in the past a Christian community might gather around the bereaved to offer support in their grief at an unexpected death, today support and hope are even more needed during a lengthening dying process!

1900			
Order	Cause of Death	% All Deaths	Deaths per 100,000
	All causes	100.0%	1,719.1
1	Influenza, pneumonia	11.8%	202.2
2	Tuberculosis (all varieties) . .	11.3%	194.4
3	Gastroenteritis	8.3%	142.7
4	Heart disease	8.0%	137.4
5	Strokes	6.2%	106.9
6	Chronic nephritis	4.7%	81.0
7	Accidents	4.2%	72.3
8	Cancer.	3.7%	64.0
	All others	41.8%	718.9

1972			
Order	Cause of Death	% All Deaths	Deaths per 100,000
	All causes	100.0%	942.2
1	Heart disease	38.3%	361.3
2	Cancer.	17.7%	166.6
3	Strokes	10.7%	100.9
4	Accidents	5.8%	54.6
5	Influenza, pneumonia	3.1%	29.4
	All others	24.4%	229.4

Figure 1. Major Causes of Death in the United States.

Adapted from *Monthly Vital Statistics Reports*, 1976, U.S. Public Health Service, printed by the U.S. Government Printing Office.

The changes in the lifespan and causes of death in our society have led to other changes, which also deepen the need for support from a caring community. Many writers have pointed out that "dying is largely done for us by the old, tucked away, out of sight," and that "people don't die at home, as they used to."[1] Kübler-Ross, whose pioneering work focused medical interest on care of the terminally ill, suggests that one reason it is so hard to die is that "most people in our society die in a hospital. This, in itself, is one of the primary reasons that dying is so hard." She points out further that, from a sociological point of view, the hospital is a depersonalizing institution not set up to meet the human needs of persons who are beyond medical help.[2] In fact, as we'll see in later chapters, the dying patient represents "failure" to many in the medical professions, who are technically superb at healing, but unable to help the human being who cannot be healed. Hospitals, generally, minister to the body, not to the whole person.[3]

The age factor and the tendency to locate care in hospital settings combine to isolate many terminally ill individuals from the settings and relationships which have made their lives meaningful. In many care settings medical personnel discourage visits from family and friends. Personal clothing, and the possessions that have meaning to the individual, are ruled out for medical (sterile) reasons, as well as for the efficient operation of the medical facility. But while there may be good reason from the point of view of institutional convenience to isolate a patient, the impact on the individual is destructive. Sociologist Erving Goffman has written of a "stripping process" by which institutions fit individuals into their systems and procedures, and effectively deny the individual a personal sense of identity, of control, and of status. The pressures imposed by the prospect of dying are great, even in ideal situations. The hospitalization of the terminally ill in our society makes the pressures even more intense, and deepens the need for support from a caring community.

Other cultural changes have their impact. Today the "family" is in most cases a nuclear unit: a small unit made up of one or two parents and their children, or of an older couple who live only with each other. While the extended family may not be emotionally separated, this small unit is geographically isolated. This means that a heavy emotional load is placed on just a few individuals when emergencies or critical situations arise. Often, when the family unit is small, the load is too great to be borne. Even when it might be better, for example, for a terminally ill individual to die at home, it's possible that the emotional impact, or the needs for physical care of the patient, may be too great for the shrunken family unit to bear.

Along with other cultural changes, the past decades have seen a shifting of values. Roy and Jane Nichols describe ours as a society which is "defiant about death; which reveres youth so highly; which conceals the aged and the ill in institutions; which portrays death in the media as tragic, horrible, unlawful, unwanted, seldom as peaceful or wanted; which wants everything so comfortable and so convenient; which attempts to manipulate and control its total environment; in that kind of society death is frequently interpreted as an insult, an intruder, as unnecessary, as superimposed on life."[4]

In this context death is often viewed as someone's fault, and terminal illness brings with it a peculiar sense of guilt. For believers this guilt may take the form of questioning what sin or sins were committed, or of shame for lack of faith ("If I only had enough faith, I'd be healed"). But it is important to realize that the sense of guilt and shame associated with illness and death is essentially cultural, not just religious. Even the medical personnel involved, devoted to healing, will often feel a sense of guilt about what was done or left undone that "might have" possibly made a difference.

Death has never been a pleasant or welcomed visitor. But today the kinds of changes in our society which we've sketched here make the process of dying even more traumatic. And these changes make the need for support from a caring community of brothers and sisters, which the Church of Christ *is,* more deeply needed than ever before.

And yet the very pressures that deepen the need also tend to isolate the terminally ill from others!

Isolation

Paul Johnson, co-author of this book, is a physician and surgeon in Seattle, Washington. For many years he has worked with persons with terminal illnesses, and developed a sensitivity to their needs and many practical approaches to helping. Now Paul has himself experienced life-threatening cancer, and has come to know personally the impact of such an illness. Recently he talked about some of the feelings of isolation that develop, and their causes.

"Partly it was embarrassment. All of a sudden I was different; someone somehow inferior, abnormal. Then, too, just as suddenly, I was the focus of attention. But it was a strange kind of attention. Not really personal, but impersonal, as I was the object of tests and examinations and all sorts of sterile routines. All of this seemed aimed at making me pull back, within myself, away from relationships which were now impersonal and professional rather than personal and caring.

"There was also a sense of oppression; of fear, or anxiety, that could easily have become depression. And with this there was the disease itself, that brought nausea and pain and many other kinds of discomfort. This was heightened by the side effects of medication, especially chemotherapy. I felt so rotten that often I wanted to be isolated.

"I can also recall feeling very different from others at times. Sometimes small talk really bothered me. There were so many things that seemed more important to be involved in. My priorities had shifted, and things which were a normal and valid part of other people's lives no longer were important to me.

"And then, with it all, there was the pull toward self-pity.

"All these very personal pressures seemed struggling to isolate me from others."

Paul experienced some of the inner pressures that make it hard for individuals to work through terminal illness in a context of supportive relationships. But he also suggests from personal experience many of the factors that researchers have pointed out; pressures which drive family, doctors, friends, and others in the community away from the ill person.

"Most people do not know what to say to a person, or how to relate to him. In fact many fear the disease, feeling that somehow, whatever the illness, it may be contagious. Many people in our society also do not want to face the reality of death.... They've had no close contact with death, and seem bent on denying its personal possibility.

"And of course there are the normal pressures on everyone: not enough time, and a desire not to get involved.

"Finally, all too often people aren't emotionally stable enough themselves to walk through the experience with someone who suffers from a terminal illness."

It's important as we go on to be sensitive to the intensely personal impact on individuals of the cultural factors we've described. Dying has never been easy. But our society has stretched out the dying process. Our society has increasingly isolated the terminally ill from the relationships in which they might find support, while the values and life patterns in our society tend to drive members of the community away from the individual. In fact, the "side effects" of dying can be of far greater threat to the individual than death itself.

Impact on the Dying

What are the side effects of dying? They are threats to the very identity and sense of self-worth of the individual; threats that from a Christian perspective are extremely serious.

Threat to the self-system. Many researchers have pointed out ways that serious illnesses constitute a threat to the individual self-system. "The thrust of our culture is directed toward physical perfection and health," observes Sharon Roberts of the California State University School of Nursing. "It's no wonder people are taken off guard when the impact of illness manifests itself. Suddenly there exists a tremendous threat to the individual's internal being."[5] Her point is that a person who suddenly finds himself unable to do what he is used to doing feels diminished even to the point of losing a personal sense of significant identity.

This is not surprising in a society where identity is usually ascribed by occupation or accomplishment. "Who are you?" is answered by such statements as "I'm a businessman," or "I'm a homemaker," or "I'm a Sunday School teacher." The individual's sense of identity is rooted in what he or she does. With serious illness comes not only the loss of many physical abilities, but often the loss of ability to accomplish the job which provided the individual's sense of identity.

We can add to this the impact of the hospital, which "embraces the individual totally and provides procedures and rituals which strip the person of his autonomy, identity, and his distinguishable separate status."⁶ Often even the name is lost, and the individual becomes "the patient in bed three" or "the woman in 206."

Threat to security. There are also many threats to the individual's sense of security. Often these threats relate to the failure of medical personnel to explain procedures or to give information on life-threatening illnesses.

Many studies of doctors' attitudes have been made, which reveal the fear that if they speak honestly the patient might not be able to take it. At the same time other studies have shown that both healthy individuals and the ill would definitely prefer to be told the truth about their diagnosis.

The attempt to "protect" usually adds to the insecurity of the individual, and leads to a distortion of the relationships he or she has with others. Glasser and Strauss in the late 60s described various kinds of awareness of dying and their impact on the ill person. The four states described were:

(1) Closed awareness. Others know the individual has a terminal illness, but the patient himself does not. This leads to evasion and lying about the expected future. In this situation the patient normally will sense that something is wrong, stress and insecurity will build, and yet the patient will be

unable to penetrate the barrier of deceit, or build significant supportive relationships with others.

(2) Suspected awareness. This is a middle state between knowledge and ignorance. The individual suspects he may die, but does not know for sure. He or she begins to watch for clues, tries to catch others off guard, and in general seeks to find out indirectly what others are unwilling to share directly. This particular state of awareness is terribly destructive of security, causing great swings of emotion between fear and hope. Once again, this state also limits significant communication and support.

(3) Pretense. In this awareness state, both the patient and others know the individual has a life-threatening illness or is in a terminal stage. Yet both tacitly agree to act as if this weren't so. The pretense itself is a great threat to security, and again blocks development of supportive relationships.

(4) Open awareness. In this state both the individual and those surrounding him or her know the seriousness of the situation. While there will be problems the individual must face and work through, the open context allows him to deal with reality, and allows those around him to be supportive and helpful.

Even though there is less threat to security in the open awareness setting, many in helping professions, and many friends of terminally ill people, persist in attempting to "protect" them.

Threat to worth and value. There are many influences in the setting of care for the terminally ill which mount serious threats to the individual's sense of worth and value. In *Toward a Sociology of Death and Dying,* Victor Marshall observes about one care facility, "On the whole, the attitude of staff toward patients and residents was marked by a benevolent maternalism, as the 'just like children' remark indicates, or as is evident in a nursing assistant's characterization of her patients: 'They're all babies. They all need care.

They like to be babied.' This attitude leads staff to adopt a pattern of high control over the status passages."[7]

In other settings attitudes of resentment appear, as many health care professionals tend to feel that caring for those who cannot be healed is a waste of time, and often display a sense of anger when patients "die on me."[8]

Such attitudes have an impact on the ill, communicating to them they no longer have value and are in essence "as good as dead."

Often even those closest to the terminally ill individual reinforce this sense of social death. Loved ones take over the tasks and the decision-making once shared with the dying person. He or she is more and more isolated from participation in the lives of others. Even areas in which he had primary responsibilities—whether areas of financial responsibility for the family, or decisions about how the family will spend time and money—are often stripped away under the impression that the individual is being helped. All too often this kind of helping communicates to the person that he or she is actually as good as dead. His contributions to the welfare of the family are no longer needed: others cope just as if he was no longer alive. And the medical care personnel treat him as a baby or a brother, not as an individual who has worth and value and still has a contribution to make to the lives of others.

It's true. Death is a natural and, for most of us, an expected part of living. The Christian can face death with a sense of confidence if not with expectation, because of our relationship with God through Jesus Christ. But the process of dying is often far worse and far more traumatic than death itself. It is in the process of dying that the individual's identity, his security, and his very sense of worth as a human being may be threatened and attacked. In our modern society, where dying has become a process rather than an event, support from a sensitive, caring community of brothers and sisters who, with wisdom and love can communicate the value of the individual to them and to God, is especially needed.

A Hospital Patient's Bill of Rights

1. The patient has the right to considerate and respectful care.

2. The patient has the right to obtain from his physician complete current information concerning his diagnosis, treatment, and prognosis in terms the patient can be reasonably expected to understand. When it is not medically advisable to give such information to the patient, the information should be made available to an appropriate person in his behalf.

3. The patient has the right to obtain from his physician information necessary to give informed consent prior to the start of any procedure and/or treatment. Except in emergencies, such information for informed consent should include, but not necessarily be limited to, the specific procedure and/or treatment, the medically significant risks involved, and the probable duration of incapacitation. Where medically significant alternatives for care or treatment exist, or when the patient requests information concerning medical alternatives, the patient has the right to such information.

4. The patient has the right to refuse treatment to the extent permitted by law and to be informed of the medical consequences of his action.

5. The patient has the right to every consideration of his privacy concerning his own medical care program.

6. The patient has the right to expect all communications and records pertaining to his care should be treated as confidential.

Figure 2. Hospital Patient's Bill of Rights.

Six of 12 items on the Hospital Patient's Bill of Rights, American Hospital Association, that have direct relevance to care of the terminally ill.

Developing Sensitivity

Certainly not everyone is insensitive to the needs of persons with terminal illness. In many hospitals adjustments are being made to treat individuals as whole persons rather than as "patients." In Paul Johnson's hospital in Seattle, visiting hours have been dropped so people can come to be with the ill person at any time. Paul and other doctors have made a number of very simple yet very important changes, such as having individuals wear their favorite clothes from home rather than wear hospital gowns. A number of items on the 1973 "Patient's Bill of Rights" published by the American Hospital Association (Figure 2) speak of the whole person and to the emotional needs which are created by life-threatening illnesses.

Yet there is still a great need for more sensitive care by medical personnel who understand the special concerns of the terminally ill and who know how to be supportive and caring. Certainly development of appropriate caring attitudes and skills is important for Christian doctors and nurses, who have a unique opportunity to communicate God's love in practical ways, and to share a dimension of hope which otherwise might be completely lacking.

There is also a great need for family members to understand what the terminally ill person may experience, and to learn how to be supportive. All too often family members act out of love, but unwisely. Their well meaning reactions can actually increase the pressures on the terminally ill rather than be supportive.

In addition, the family itself is placed under great pressures by the life-threatening illness of one of its members. These pressures normally mean that family members need to receive support as well as to give it. Not only do loved ones need to have some understanding of the impact of terminal illnesses, but they also need personal support from a caring community.

In a helpful little book, Randy Becton shares some of the ways that the church of which he is a member provided support for his family and for himself when he was stricken with cancer.

One Christian decided to look after the physical needs of my family, never coming to see me but showing how very much he loved me by looking after my loved ones. Some Christian ladies found their way to help by looking after all the needs at home for my wife. Some mothers kept my children with theirs in order to lighten my wife's load, freeing her to spend more time with me. Some Christian men decided that whatever house repairs and work were needed would be done. Others regularly found the time to give some cheerful item, card, flower, etc., as an expression of love. Still others found their ministry in the giving of money to help defray expenses.[9]

This ministry of the Church as a family to Randy's family effectively communicated love and caring to Randy as well as solved many practical problems which are so draining at such times.

Yet even more important than what we can do for those who are living through the dying process is what we can do *with* them. To be a caring person, to develop a one-on-one personal relationship in which we can be truly supportive, is both a goal and a problem for the Christian. Will a dying person want this kind of relationship? Will he want to talk about his illness, or his future? Will he reject our overtures? Will we make matters worse? What can anyone say that will really help? How can we share our faith and our lives to be of help and comfort? Our very unfamiliarity with death, its very isolation from normal patterns of life in our society, deepens our uncertainty and hesitation to become involved.

If we are to grow as Christians and as helping persons, and if our churches are to grow as caring communities, it's important to face such fears, and to learn what we *can* do. We need to clarify our understanding of and attitude toward death and dying. We need to understand and be sensitive to the fears, and the reactions, of the terminally ill. We need also to become aware of our own feelings; of the pressures on the medical personnel, the nuclear family, and brothers and sisters in neighborhood and congregation. We need to understand, so we can learn to respond in significant ways that affirm the value of the person and help him or her make passage through the valley of the shadow of death a part of his growth toward God and his full potential as a person.

In the first part of this book we'll survey basic needs which call for understanding. Then we'll go on to look specifically at the response of believers in the caring community. We'll sketch opportunities to care that arise in every community, examine personal relationships with the terminally ill, and see ways we can help create an atmosphere of hope in which life retains its meaning up to the end. We'll also look at various models of the caring community; ways that others have responded to meet the needs of the terminally ill. Finally, just before surveying resources that are available, we'll suggest a training program that can be conducted for members of a local congregation, for medical personnel, for families, or simply as preparation for dying, as a significant step toward building a caring community that is ready, as God's family, to gather around and care.

Developing Sensitivity

> Personal projects for individuals or study groups to help develop sensitivity for ministry with the terminally ill.

1.   Who was the last person in your family or congregation who died? How did the Christian community respond? What was your own involvement, and how did you feel?

2.   If you had a terminal illness, which of the following situations would you prefer: a closed awareness, suspected awareness, pretense, or open awareness setting (see pp. 16-17)? Jot down as many advantages and disadvantages of each situation for the ill person as you can.

3.   Look carefully at the "Bill of Rights" included on page 19. How would you rewrite each item, and what would you add, to have the Bill of Rights more specifically responsive to the special needs of the terminally ill, as you now understand them?

Chapter 1, Notes

1. Michael A. Simpson, *Facts of Death* (Englewood Cliffs, N.J.: Prentice-Hall, Inc., 1979), p. 4.

2. Elisabeth Kübler-Ross, ed., *Death: the Final Stage of Growth* (Englewood Cliffs, N.J.: Prentice-Hall, Inc., 1975), p. 5.

3. Laurens P. White, "Death and the Physician," in *New Meanings of Death*, ed. Herman Feifel (New York: McGraw-Hill, 1977).

4. Ray and Jan Nichols, "Funerals," in *New Meanings*, p. 92.

5. Sharon L. Roberts, *Behavioral Concepts and the Critically Ill Patient* (Englewood Cliffs, N.J.: Prentice-Hall, Inc., 1976), p. 187.

6. Dr. Hans O. Mauksch, "The Organizational Context of Dying," in *New Meanings*, p. 16.

7. Victor W. Marshall, "Organizational Features of Terminal Status Passage in Residential Facilities for the Aged," in *Toward a Sociology of Death and Dying*, ed. Lyn H. Lofland (Beverly Hills, Ca.: Sage Publications, 1976), p. 130.

8. Elisabeth Kübler-Ross, *On Death and Dying* (New York: Macmillan Co., 1969), p. 252.

9. Randy Becton, *The Gift of Life* (Abilene, Tex.: Quality Publications, 1979), p. 51.

Chapter 2

The Valley of the Shadow

*T*he day I finished writing *Creative Bible Teaching* my mother died. I got the phone call from my sister. I sat back down at my typewriter and finished the last few sentences of the last chapter. And then I typed the dedication that you can read there today:

> To my parents,
> Vivian and Charlotte Richards
> whose quiet living of God's Word
> has proven to be His creative
> force in my life.

The next day I took Paul, my nine-year-old son, and drove from Chicago back to my childhood home in Michigan.

When I turned into the driveway my dad was standing out by the garage. It was then the first tears came. He looked so stooped and alone.

The day after was the funeral. My mother had told me some years before an Old Testament passage she wanted used at her funeral. I took her worn Bible, and looked through it till I found the verses she'd marked.

So the first funeral I preached was my mother's. But there were no tears then. Instead there was a great surge of joy as I stood there, with relatives and friends, and looked over toward the body in the casket realizing, with them, that my mother was not there. She was with the Lord whom she loved.

But then, at the cemetery, the tears came again. As the casket was lowered into the ground a great sense of sorrow and loss flooded over me, and I reached out to touch my dad, knowing how empty his life would be.

Late that night Paul, sleeping with me in the upstairs bedroom that had been mine as a child, began to sob. He'd been quiet and withdrawn during the last few days. He'd refused to go to the funeral home for the viewing. At the funeral he sat there, motionless and just a little pale, with my sister and the other relatives. Now, at last, he cried heartbrokenly. And now, at last, I could hug him and explain that I'd brought him with me to Michigan just so he could cry. He'd been very close to his grandparents. And he needed to experience the sorrow that death brings...and to affirm the hope that we as Christians have.

Death

It's hard for us to work through to a biblical understanding of death. Especially because we tend to explore death's reality only when tragedy is upon us.

Much of the literature today on death and dying speaks of, or implies, that a calm acceptance is the final and, to the writers, the ideal response to death. Kübler-Ross describes acceptance as a "final stage" in the dying process, and calls it "not a happy stage, but neither is it unhappy. It's devoid of feelings but it's not resignation, it's really a victory."[1]

Many who have researched death and dying are carefully descriptive; they refrain from making judgments on how death ought to be perceived. Others approach death philosophically, stressing that it is part of the natural order of the universe. While not welcomed, death must be accepted. And, because death is inevitable, facing it with quiet courage is seen, as by Kübler-Ross, as something of a victory.

This perspective accords with the approach of the Greeks who gave us our New Testament words for death.[2] The primary word, *thanatos*, expresses man's mortality and pictures an end to all life's activities. Because death involves the end of existence, it was viewed with some horror. Yet all men are subject to death; it is inevitable and must ultimately be faced.

One of the responses of the Greeks to death was to stress enjoyment of life. "'Let us eat and drink, for tomorrow we die'" (1 Corinthians 15:32) was no expression of flippant disregard, but the pagan's affirmation of the belief that he must make the most of his present existence, for the pleasures of the moment were the only pleasures available to him.

While the Greeks always honored a good death (such as a hero's death in battle, or one fearlessly facing his end), the philosophers introduced a new perspective. Death cannot be known, so why should it be feared? If we accept the natural inevitability of our death and realize that we are all in the process of dying, we will overcome fear. A calm readiness to accept what must be is the appropriate end to a good man's life, and such a death becomes a triumph.

It's not surprising that many today, including Christians, hold a similar ideal. Believers, sustained by the knowledge of an immortality that the pagan Greeks never dreamed of, are supposed to face death not only with calm but even with joy.

Yet Scripture does not sound that note of happy eagerness. Nor does the Bible hold out the ideal of calm that we sometimes think Christians ought to feel. Both Old and New Testaments picture death as an enemy, not a friend.

Valley of the Shadow

We catch a glimpse of Scripture's portrayal of death in David's famous shepherd's psalm. Death is a shadow falling

on a person passing through a deep valley. In that valley it is
appropriate to fear. Only the assurance of God's presence,
shepherding His beloved sheep through even this experience,
can bring comfort and release from fear (Psalm 23:4).

Hezekiah's response to the threat of death while in the
"prime of my life" is not uncommon: he mourned and wept
and, when he recovered, saw in his restoration a love from
God which "kept me from the pit of destruction" (cf. Isaiah
38:9-20). Many psalms contain appeals for deliverance from
death. Long life is satisfying (Psalm 91:16); to be cut off
from life is tragedy (cf. Psalm 6:3, 8-10). Psalm 90 speaks
powerfully of man's mortality, and asks not only that God
might have compassion during the brief 70 or 80 years of life
allotted, but also that God might

> Teach us to number our days aright,
>   that we may gain a heart of wisdom.
> Psalm 90:12

The believer will find comfort in the valley in the presence
and love of God. But there is no question that, as death approaches, the valley we enter is dark.

It is very wrong to treat death lightly. Or to blithely
assume as death approaches that our brother or sister must be
eager to be with the Lord. Death is, and always has been, an
enemy. If we Christians approach death with a strange confidence, it's not because we welcome it. It's because we have a
personal relationship with God like the one expressed in
Psalm 73:

> Yet I am always with you;
>   you hold me by my right hand.
> You guide me with your counsel,
>   and afterward you will take me into glory.
> Whom have I in heaven but you?
>   And being with you, I desire nothing
>   on earth.

My flesh and my heart may fail,
but God is the strength of my heart
and my portion forever.
                    Psalm 73:23-26

The enemy. Corinthians clearly portrays death as an enemy. In fact, death is "the last enemy to be destroyed" when Christ begins to reign (1 Corinthians 15:26). We are hardly justified in presenting death as a friend when Scripture identifies it as our enemy, and God's.

The great affirmation of the New Testament is that God has dealt with this enemy in principle, and one day soon will deal with death in fact. We have the gospel promise of resurrection: our imperfection, our separation from our loved ones, our alienation from God, will be set aside "in a flash, in the twinkling of an eye, at the last trumpet."

Describing that final victory Scripture conveys God's great commitment:

> The trumpet will sound, the dead will be raised imperishable, and we will be changed. For the perishable must clothe itself with the imperishable, and the mortal with immortality. When the perishable has been clothed with the imperishable, and the mortal with immortality, then the saying that is written will come true: "Death has been swallowed up in victory." 1 Corinthians 15:52-54

But the day of victory is ahead. It is not yet here. And so we who are perishable, mortal, and deeply aware of our mortality, must face death. We can face death in faith, freed from a bondage that brings terror (cf. Hebrews 2:14,15), but we will face death sadly, recognizing in it an enemy that Christ alone can, and one day will, forever put away.

Death vs. life. Actually, it's appropriate that the Christian focus on life as the realm of hope rather than on death.

God's warning to Adam and Eve in the garden was a presentation of life, contrasted with a choice that would lead to death. Throughout Scripture where life and death are contrasted, death is always the one from which we're to turn away.

"See," Moses proclaimed, "I set before you today life and prosperity, death and destruction" (Deuteronomy 30:15). And Israel was urged to choose life.

And as Paul explains, "sin entered the world through one man, and death through sin, and in this way death came to all men" (Romans 5:12). Death and sin are brothers.

So death is not a friend of man. Death is an enemy. Death crept into our experience with sin, and physical death, with its cutting off of all relationships in the physical universe, is an appropriate picture of the spiritual impact of sin, which shatters our relationship with God and other persons and corrupts the image of Himself which God planned for the human personality. Theologically, death is so intimately entwined with our sinful condition, both as a result of sin and as an evidence of its relationship-destroying power, that we can never lightly view its approach or even welcome death as a doorway to Eternity.

Yes, we will pass through death and enter Jesus' presence. But the doorway is one of darkness and not light; a final reminder of our mortality and our need for deliverance.

Eternal life. The Bible focuses our attention on life, not death. And here we have the greatest of promises. Jesus, through His suffering of a death which the Bible says was *for* us (1 Corinthians 15:3f.; Romans 4:25; Romans 5:6f.; 1 Peter 3:18; Colossians 1:22; etc.), reconciled us to God. In raising Christ to new life, the power of sin was broken. While the mortal in us will suffer a physical death, there is also an immortal dimension which cannot be destroyed. "You have been born again," Peter explains, "not of perishable seed, but of imperishable, through the living and enduring word of God" (1 Peter 1:23).

Relationship with God through Christ brings us a life which death cannot extinguish. And so the Bible speaks of life that is both eternal and our present possession; to affirm not only our continued self-conscious existence as persons, but also to affirm a total healing of our personality and a perfected relationship with God. "God so loved the world," Jesus taught, "that he gave his one and only Son, that whoever believes in him shall not perish but have eternal life" (John 3:16).

Death still holds its mysteries. "What we will be has not yet been made known," John says. But "now we *are* children of God...[And] we know that when he appears, we shall be like him, for we shall see him as he is" (1 John 3:2).

It is confidence in our relationship with God, and in His great gift of eternal life, which makes the experience of death different for the believer. We do not view death as any less an enemy, for death is God's enemy, too. But we are able to see death as a defeated enemy. We realize that "if we live, we live to the Lord; and if we die, we die to the Lord. So, whether we live or die, we belong to the Lord" (Romans 14:8). The fact that death cannot threaten our relationship with God is the key to a Christian approach to death and dying.

We need not welcome death, or even be calm in its presence. We can acknowledge our fears, our disappointments, all the uncertainty associated with meeting any enemy face to face. And we can still find great comfort and assurance in God's personal commitment to us as His children:

> ...neither death nor life, neither angels nor demons, neither the present nor the future, nor any powers, neither height nor depth, nor anything else in all creation, will be able to separate us from the love of God that is in Christ Jesus our Lord. Romans 8:38,39.

Shared Perspectives

A sensitivity to the Bible's portrayal of death is important in a caring ministry with the terminally ill. Much of our uncertainty and discomfort in relating to the terminally ill comes because the nature of death is such a stranger to us. We are not sure what we should expect from the dying person. And we lack the biblical framework in which to evaluate our own feelings and responses. By developing a biblical understanding of death as an enemy which although defeated by Christ is still a dark doorway into eternity, we're better able to relate to the dying. We are more comfortable in dealing with the dying, and we are much more able to be supportive. Here are just a few of the areas where understanding death as an enemy helps us acquire a healthy perspective.

Acceptance. Even those who are not Christians tend to have expectations as to how a person ought to die. The non-Christian may tend to feel that death should be faced "like a man." Or with gratitude for a full life. The believer may tend to think the individual should be eager to be with the Lord, or even happy to die. Any feelings of fear or disappointment or anger, which are all natural responses to the grim announcement that life is likely to end soon, may be rejected.

There's consistent testimony in the literature on death, as well as from the personal experiences of countless generations of believers, that those with a meaningful faith do meet death with a calm and courageous hope. This is something that Paul Johnson has observed in his thirty years as a Christian surgeon. But we should not expect that either calm or joyful expectancy will mark the months of dying. Instead we should expect the message of death to be experienced as a threat. We should expect, and accept, a variety of emotions and reactions as the shadows deepen.

It's important when we minister to the terminally ill to accept the dying person's feelings.

Acceptance has a significant impact on communication. When a person senses that what he is doing or saying is not acceptable—that we are judging him—he's forced to defend himself against us. He puts up barriers, and hides his true thoughts and feelings. Locking the thoughts and feelings inside, sensing the condemnation, the individual is blocked from working the feelings through.

On the other hand, when an individual senses that we do not judge or condemn but understand and accept his feelings, that person is freed to share. In the sharing, feelings can be explored and understood, and words of comfort can be heard.

It's very important that we move into ministry with the dying without embarrassment at the feelings which they may express and without a judgmental attitude. We need to realize that the believer can maintain a steadfast hope in God and still experience great turmoil in the face of death. After all, Christ Himself did not approach death lightly. Scripture tells us that at Gethsemane "he began to be sorrowful and troubled." He told his disciples, "'My soul is overwhelmed with sorrow to the point of death.'" Three times He prayed in anguish to the Father that the cup about to be poured for Him—death, and all that His death entailed—might be taken from Him (cf. Matthew 26:36-44). Jesus knew full well what was waiting for Him beyond death's portal. He had told His disciples of His coming resurrection. He knew that He would soon be caught up into glory with the Father. He was aware that by His death our salvation would be accomplished. But in spite of all the joy that He knew was set before Him, the cross was something to be endured rather than welcomed (Hebrews 12:2).

Certainly our death lacks the meaning, and the many elements, of Christ's. But just as certainly we who are so mortal and comparatively so weak in faith can hardly be blamed if the approach of death overwhelms us with sorrow, even as it did Jesus.

Comfort. It's important to recognize death as an enemy which rightly causes us times of anguish and sorrow. It is also important to understand the nature of the comfort which we can offer to those who are dying.

Most persons who are dying are not deeply concerned about the specific shape of eternity. And we should not speak dogmatically, with too great an assurance that the picture we paint actually represents what God has in store. It's very important to keep in mind John's statement: "Dear friends, now we are children of God, and what we will be has not yet been made known" (1 John 3:2). We may not know what lies ahead, but we know that we are God's children now. We know we have an intimate family relationship with the Lord. Thus we can be assured of His constant care, today.

There are, of course, clues to eternity in Scripture. We know that personal, self-conscious existence continues beyond the grave. Jesus' pictures of life beyond death (Luke 16:19-31), His confident expectation that historic individuals will be raised and retain their identity (Luke 11:29-32), His promise to the dying thief that that day they would be together in paradise (Luke 23:43)—these and many other passages make the continuation of the personality a clear and assured fact of revelation.

Pictures in Scripture of the resurrected Jesus add more clues. John says that while we do not really know the shape of eternity, "we shall be like him, for we shall see him as he is" (1 John 3:2b). Paul in Corinthians speaks of Christ as the first fruits: we who follow will share fully in His resurrection. But questions of "How are the dead raised?" and "With what kind of body will they come?" are set aside. There is a correspondence between that which we are now and that which we will be. But there will also be a transformation. The seed planted in the ground will burst forth in the sunlight as a new planting. "The body that is sown is perishable, it is raised imperishable; it is sown in dishonor, it is raised in glory; it is sown in weakness, it is raised in power; it is sown a natural body, it is raised a spiritual body" (1 Corinthians 15:35ff).

Actually, it's appropriate to leave the future in God's hands. We look around us at the distortions which sin has brought to our present world and into our own lives, and we realize that God must have something far better for us. We live and we die in this hope. But, as Paul points out in a beautiful passage in Romans, a hope which is seen and possessed is no longer hope. And faith calls us today to live in hope, with our expectation focused on God.

"The creation waits in eager expectation for the sons of God to be revealed," Paul writes. And goes on to affirm:

> We know that the whole creation has been groaning as in the pains of childbirth right up to the present time. Not only so, but we ourselves, who have the firstfruits of the Spirit, groan inwardly as we wait eagerly for our adoption as sons, the redemption of our bodies. For in this hope we were saved. But hope that is seen is no hope at all. Who hopes for what he already has? But if we hope for what we do not yet have, we wait for it patiently. Romans 8:19,22-25

It's important to note here that the hope of which Paul speaks is not death, nor is death its doorway. The hope is the time coming when God will set all things right: when resurrection will bring us all to the perfection He has planned for us, and when death's last taint will have been purged from the very universe itself.

And so the Bible does hint at what awaits us. But it is as if a curtain was drawn back just enough for us to glimpse the splendor that lies beyond the shadow realm of death. The full shape of what awaits us is not disclosed.

This is vital to understand, because it is not portraits of eternity that bring comfort to the dying. The key to comfort is not the knowledge of what lies ahead, but the affirmation of God's continuing love and constant presence.

"Neither death nor life, neither angels nor demons,
neither the present nor the future...." nothing in
the whole of creation or in the depths of despair...
"will be able to separate us from the love of God
that is in Christ Jesus our Lord." Romans 8:38-39

God has said,
    "Never will I leave you;
    never will I forsake you."
                    Hebrews 13:5

Even though I walk
    through the valley of the shadow of death,
I will fear no evil,
    for you are with me;
your rod and your staff,
    they comfort me.
                    Psalm 23:4

These are the words that bring comfort. These are the great
affirmations of our faith with which we can support our
brothers and sisters who are walking in the valley.

There is another aspect of comfort which is important
for us to grasp. The roots of comfort are the assurance that
we are not abandoned; that we are loved and valued, and that
God draws close to walk the valley with us. How do we communicate this kind of comfort?

First, by affirmation. We need to assure our brothers
and sisters of God's love. We need to speak together of the
continuing love of God and, if there are times when a person
wants to be encouraged from Scripture, the most appropriate
passages to choose are those which affirm God's love.

Second, and at times far more important, we need to be
agents through which God's love and His presence are
mediated. We need to be the family, gathered around. By our
presence, by a touch, by the warmth of a familiar voice, we
let a person know in unmistakable ways that he is valued and

loved. We let a person know that when all the things that he once *did* to make himself important are stripped away, he is loved as a significant member of God's Family. By the love of the Family gathered around, we communicate the reality of a God who also hovers near, to shepherd His loved one through the darkness of the valley of the shadow of death.

Inevitability. One of the first reactions to the diagnosis of a life-threatening illness is likely to be, "Why me?" This is also often accompanied by a sense of undifferentiated guilt. There may be nothing the individual has done that he or she can pinpoint as a reason for God cutting short the life, but still feelings of guilt surge.

Once again a biblical perspective on death helps us to understand and to respond. Death is associated with sin. So is guilt. The flood of feelings that may come are simply evidence of the linkage of these great enemies of man.

But the sense of guilt and the questions of "Why me?" which the threat of death arouses point up other issues. Is death a specific punishment? What are the reasons why one person is cut off and another lives a long life? It should be abundantly clear that these are the kinds of questions none of us can answer. There is no biblical necessity to portray God as One who actively selects the cutting off of a person's days. At the same time it's clear that God does exercise sovereign rule over all things. He *could* act to change our fate. He *can* act to interrupt the natural course of events today. But in most cases God will not do so. Like those who are not children of God, His loved ones, too, live in a tangled universe which has been warped and twisted by sin. We, too, experience the suffering which imperfection and evil bring. For most of us, the "Why?" questions will remain unanswered. For most of us, the sudden unexplainable remission of the cancer, or miraculous restoration of the heart, will not be a part of God's plan. For most of us, the enemy will have to be faced, often too soon. And, when our times of denial and doubt have passed, we will find in Christ the grace to follow Peter's prescription for those who "suffer according to God's will." We will "commit [ourselves] to [our] faithful Creator and continue to do good" (1 Peter 4:19).

What is important here as we think of the inevitability of death is to recognize several forms that a caring ministry can take as a person with the terminal illness lives through the dying process.

Timing. While death is inevitable for all except the final generation (1 Thessalonians 4:13-18), the date of any individual's death is not. As the first "why's" are asked, the caring community can and should gather around the individual with prayer to God for healing. "You do not have, because you do not ask God," James chides the community of Jewish believers at Jerusalem (James 4:2). They had forgotten to trust themselves as children to a loving Father, and to bring everything to Him.

It's always appropriate to bring needs to God. He is involved in our joys; He is moved by our sorrows. Over and over Scripture affirms that God values us supremely. Bringing our needs and our requests to God is something He desires, and it is an important way to affirm the value of the possibly dying individual at a time when his or her sense of worth is most threatened.

God may choose to answer the prayer for healing. Then the caring community will rejoice with the one who has been restored. Or God may choose not to intervene. And then the individual and the community will find the grace to affirm His faithfulness in spite of the apparent silence.

Faith healing. At some time in the dying process there is likely to be an intrusion from those whose faith in God is expressed by the firm conviction that God does heal—if only we have sufficient faith. This is particularly likely if the dying person is relatively young, and the terminal illness lengthy.

On the one hand we want to affirm that God *can* heal. The Christian's faith is firmly fixed on a God who has intervened in history to act decisively in man's world. While God normally works through natural processes, the biblical picture of miracles makes us confident that God is not under bondage to natural law.

On the other hand, we want to be just as clear in stating that God does not limit His own freedom of action by chaining Himself to the amount or quality of a human being's "faith." It is a complete misunderstanding of faith to view it as a work which can compel God to act according to *our* will.

In fact, faith is always a response to God's self-revelation. God has spoken through His Word; we respond with trust and obedience, and this kind of faith guides us into our new life with Him. God speaks to us through His Spirit; we sense His guidance as we come to Him in prayer, and when the Spirit's confirmation is given, we know that He has heard and will answer our prayer. This Spirit-given awareness of God's confirmation is the secret of believing prayer, and helps us understand such passages as "all things you ask in prayer, believing, you shall receive" (Matthew 21:22, NASB). God is not telling us that belief is a *condition* we must meet before He'll answer. Instead God is reassuring us that, as we ask in His will, His Spirit will give the confirmation, and we will know before He answers that He has heard.

We want to be extremely careful in ministering to the terminally ill that we never suggest the illness or its progress is their fault. "If only you had enough faith," some suggest, "you would be healed." Or they insist excitedly, "You're healed! Just stand up now and claim the healing!" But when the person who is ill is not healed, the waves of guilt wash back, and God appears to be a distant, disapproving tyrant who withholds love because His child has failed to perform up to His demanding standards.

The tragedy of this approach to healing is that, just when the believer most needs assurance of God's love and presence, others distort God into a completely different Person than He is. At a time when the individual feels most weak, and most in need of grace to help, this approch demands great strength as the price of acceptance and love. How good to know that God is *not* that kind of Person. How good to know that His love for us is unconditional; that He remembers our frame, that we are dust, and never withdraws His love from us.

Even the Apostle Paul, whose faith no one would doubt, demonstrated in his own life that healing is not guaranteed to any of us. "There was given me a thorn in my flesh, a messenger of Satan, to torment me," Paul reports in 2 Corinthians. Knowing that God could intervene, Paul brought the illness to Him in prayer. "Three times I pleaded with the Lord to take it away from me." But no confirming Word came from the Spirit. Instead the request was refused. But God did speak! "He said to me, 'My grace is sufficient for you, for my power is made perfect in weakness'" (2 Corinthians 12:7-10).

This is the perspective we can bring to those with terminal illnesses when the prayers we first offer are unanswered. God's "no" never comes harshly, but always with the promise of grace.

That grace will be sufficient.

God's power will be with us, however great our weakness.

Death with dignity. The inevitability of death for those whose terminal illness brings them to the brink raises another question. How long should the spark of life be preserved? Death is an enemy. But should death be put off at all costs?

Modern medical technology has advanced to the point where an individual's body can be kept breathing and his heart beating long past all hope of recovery—and long after the person would have died had unusual means to preserve life not been used.

This practice has been increasingly attacked as an unnecessary cause of suffering for the dying person and for the family. Increasingly individuals have insisted on the right to

To my family, friends, physician, lawyer and clergyman:

I believe that each individual person is created by God our Father in love and that God retains a loving relationship to each person throughout human life and eternity.

I believe that Jesus Christ lived, suffered, and died for me and that his suffering, death and resurrection prefigure and make possible the death-resurrection process which I now anticipate.

I believe that each person's worth and dignity derives from the relationship of love in Christ that God has for each individual person, and not from one's usefulness or effectiveness in society.

I believe that God Our Father has entrusted to me a shared dominion with him over my earthly existence so that I am bound to use ordinary means to preserve my life but I am free to refuse extraordinary means to prolong my life.

I believe that through death life is not taken away but merely changed, and though I may experience fear, suffering, and sorrow by the grace of the Holy Spirit, I hope to accept death as a free human act which enables me to surrender this life and to be united with God for eternity.

Because of my belief:

I, _____

request that I be informed as death approaches so that I may continue to prepare for the full encounter with Christ through the help of the sacraments and the consolation and prayers of my family and friends.

I request that, if possible, I be consulted concerning the medical procedures which might be used to prolong my life as death approaches. If I can no longer take part in decisions concerning my own future and there is no reasonable expectation of my recovery from physical and mental disability, I request that no extraordinary means be used to prolong my life.

I request, though I wish to join my suffering to the suffering of Jesus so I may be united fully with him in the act of death-resurrection, that my pain, if unbearable, be alleviated. However, no means should be used with the intention of shortening my life.

I request, because I am a sinner and in need of reconciliation and because my faith, hope, and love may not overcome all fear and doubt, that my family, friends and the whole Christian community join me in prayer and mortification as I prepare for the great personal act of dying.

Finally, I request that after my death, my family, my friends, and the whole Christian community pray for me, and rejoice with me because of the mercy and love of the Trinity, with whom I hope to be united for all eternity.

Signed _____

Figure 3. The Christian Affirmation of Life.
This statement was developed by the Catholic Hospital Association.

To any and all doctors, hospitals, health personnel and others treating me during my final illness:

I _____ hereby make this statement in the presence of witnesses, to declare and record my express wish and desire that: in the event, due to illness or accident, that my condition becomes terminal and without reasonable hope of recovery, then I do not wish to be kept alive by the use of drugs, treatments or machine. I wish to receive adequate medication for proper control of my symptoms, but nothing beyond what is necessary for that purpose. I hereby specifically withdraw my consent for any such primarily life-sustaining treatment, and this withdrawal of my consent shall continue unless and until I revoke it in writing. Should I, in the course of my illness, subsequently become legally incompetent or unable to communicate my wishes to those treating me, then this document should be considered as continuing to withdraw my consent to any further treatment not directed primarily at symptom relief. Any and all doctors, nurses, hospitals and institutions that honour my wishes and intentions as expressed in this document, are hereby formally held free from any and all liability on behalf of myself, my heirs, successors and assigns.

Signed _____
Dated _____

Witnesses: _____   _____

Figure 4. Refusal of Consent for Life-Prolonging Procedures.
This typical form is designed to deal with possible legal questions raised by failure to use life-prolonging means.

die with dignity when death's inevitability has been established. Figures 3 and 4 show forms which have been developed to help deal with this issue.

Confidence. One of the consistent themes of Scripture is
that we can have a confidence and peace which are not based
on knowledge of the future in the context of personal relationship with God. We can be assured of the kind of Person
He is, for God has revealed Himself to us in Scripture and in
Jesus. We can be utterly confident of God's commitment to
us, for "He who did not spare his own Son, but gave him up
for us all—how will he not also, along with him, graciously
give us all things?" (Romans 8:32).

There are tendencies to try to anchor the confidence of
the dying in something other than relationship with God.
Recently a number of books and articles have been written
reporting supposed "beyond death" experiences. These
writers offer a hope based on reports of what individuals say
they have seen when they "died." In a helpful discussion of
this "Lazarus Syndrome," Michael Simpson observes that
while the "similarities [of the reports] are challenging," they
provide "no evidence of the quality of life after death." He
adds,

> It is, however, likely that many of the states share a
> tendency toward delirium, a state in which the brain
> and mind are temporarily out of contact with reality
> and more disposed to perceive images whose con-
> tent is determined by one's psychological condition.
> There are indeed more convincing psychological
> reasons to account for these experiences, with a
> strong component of romantic wish-fulfillment; a
> variety of well-recognized psychological defense
> mechanisms would produce similar phenomena. It
> is intriguing that the experiences seem to depend
> more on how serious and hopeless the dying people

perceive their condition to be than on any objective assessment of their peril.[3]

The Christian's confidence in the face of death is ultimately rooted in the conviction that God is a trustworthy Person. The love given to us in Jesus is the one steadfast anchor for that hope.

This confidence is shared by the whole family of faith and is, ultimately, the greatest gift the caring community can bring to personal relationships with the terminally ill.

As God remains steadfast in His loyalty to the dying, so the caring community too remains loyal.

As God commits Himself to stay by His child in every extremity, so we commit ourselves to stay with our brother or sister until the end.

As God understands our frailties and weaknesses and fears, we too understand the anguish that can override all defenses as a person faces the final enemy. We understand. We accept. And we continue to value and to care.

Together, through it all, we affirm as a community of faith that God will be victorious, even over death. We believe wholeheartedly that the separation from our loved ones that tears at our hearts will, despite everything, be for a short time only.

One day the trumpet of God will sound.

One day Jesus will be revealed.

The dead in Christ will rise first.

Then we, who are alive and remain will be caught up into the air.

There we will join the dead in Christ.

Reunited with those we love, together as a whole Family, we will meet Jesus. And so we will be with the Lord.

Forever.

Developing Sensitivity

> Personal projects for individuals or study groups to help
> develop sensitivity for ministry with the terminally ill.

1. How does viewing death as an enemy affect your idea of
    how a person with a life-threatening illness "should"
    behave?

2. The authors gave three illustrations of comforting pas-
    sages of Scripture on page 36. Can you find at least five
    more that you feel would be comforting to you?

3. What seems to you to be the most significant differences
    between "faith" as a particular set of beliefs and "faith"
    as a personal relationship? How might each dimension of
    faith be helpful to a person with a life-threatening illness?
    Which do you believe would be most important? Why?

Chapter 2, Notes

1. Elisabeth Kübler-Ross, *On Death and Dying* (New York: Macmillan
Co., 1969), p. 113.

2. See the discussion of *thanatos* in *The New International Dictionary of
New Testament Theology*, ed. Colin Brown, 3 vols. (Grand Rapids:
Zondervan, 1975), 1:430-41.

3. Michael A. Simpson, *Facts of Death* (Englewood Cliffs, N.J.:
Prentice-Hall, Inc., 1979), pp. 33, 34.

Chapter 3

Cut Off

"**I**t started when I was giving my deacons some training in terminal personality stages. One of my men said, 'Next time you visit someone going through this, I'd like to come.' So I took him with me to see Jack.

"Jack had cancer in the lower part of his body. He'd already had a colostomy, and had almost no lower body functions. We visited with him in his bathrobe, in his home. His wife was also there. This was my second or third visit, and I was just trying to relate to them.

"Jack had been president of a large corporation, and when he got cancer they ruthlessly dumped him. He had run through his insurance at this point, and used his life savings, and had practically nothing left.

"I had told my deacon to listen, but not say anything. But in the middle of it my deacon just had to witness. He said, 'Jack, you speak so openly about the shortness of the life you have left. I'm sure you've thought very much about dying. I wonder if you've prepared for your life after your death?'

"Jack stood up, livid with rage. He tottered there in his bathrobe, shaking and cursing. 'You --- ---- Christians,' he shouted. 'All you ever think about is what's going to happen to me after I die. I don't know that anything will, and I don't care. If your God is so great, why doesn't He do something about the real problems of life?'

"Enraged, Jack went on to tell us that he was leaving his wife penniless. He was leaving his daughter without a college education. He was going out with a whimper, not able to provide a thing for them. And with that he ordered us to get out.

"We got outside and I said, 'You see what can happen. You went right past the man's feelings. You mirrored your own values across to him, and assumed that your values would be his, when in fact he has a totally different structure of concern.'"

It's no wonder that we feel uncomfortable at the thought of talking with a person with a life-threatening illness. How will such a person react? How will he or she feel? What can we say or do that will really help? Certainly the deacon who accompanied Pastor Ralph Neighbour, of Houston's West Memorial Baptist Church, *wanted* to help. But he failed to be aware of the likely reactions to terminal illness. And he had not heard the many clues Jack gave to the state of his feelings.

In this chapter we want to examine common reactions to life-threatening illness. We want to become aware of common fears and worries. We want to become more sensitive to the needs of those who have discovered that they may soon be cut off from the land of the living.

Fears

Ralph's deacon, as a man deeply concerned about the eternal destiny of the dying man they were visiting, focused on what might happen to Jack after he died. He was stunned to learn that Jack didn't know what would happen to him. And that Jack didn't care! Instead Jack's fears and his anger focused on his dying, and what the dying would mean to those he left behind.

For many people, if not most, fears associated with dying are greater and more pressing than the fear of death. It's important to grasp this fact as we build relationships with those with terminal illness.

Such fears are mentioned in many different studies about death and dying. A search of the literature reveals many fears that are reported time and again. Here's a listing of the most common, drawn from many sources.
- fear of helplessness
- fear of being alone, deserted
- fear of being dead, but no one notices
- fear of pain and suffering
- fear of being a burden (two-thirds of those in one study had this fear)
- fear of humiliation (of being seen without wig, unable to control bladder, etc.)
- fear of what will happen to projects
- fear of separation from loved ones
- fear of future for loved ones left behind
- fear of punishment
- fear of impairment, of being unable to care for self
- fear of the unknown
- fear others will have to "take care of me"
- fears associated with finances
- fears over loss of emotional control, of being "unable to take it"

These fears and uncertainties are completely understandable. They lurk under the surface of every life, even if they are not expressed. The threat of death rightly produces anxiety, and raises a host of questions about the immediate future which often take personal priority over issues of eternity. Our thoughts are crowded with doubts. How long do I have? Can I keep on doing my job? How will I provide for my family? Will it mean extra work for my family? Will they have to look after me? Will I deteriorate later? Who will care for the children? The future which once seemed relatively secure is now dark and uncertain. Questions churn, often unanswered, and many times unasked.

The fact that such fears and "negative feelings" are aroused by life-threatening illnesses has led many doctors,

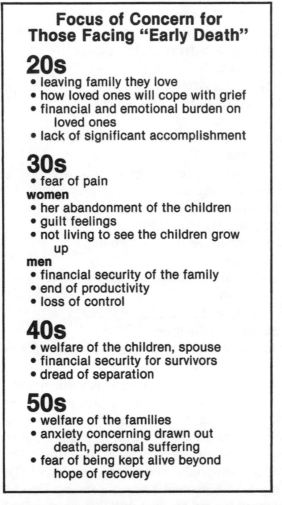

Focus of Concern for Those Facing "Early Death"

20s
- leaving family they love
- how loved ones will cope with grief
- financial and emotional burden on loved ones
- lack of significant accomplishment

30s
- fear of pain

women
- her abandonment of the children
- guilt feelings
- not living to see the children grow up

men
- financial security of the family
- end of productivity
- loss of control

40s
- welfare of the children, spouse
- financial security for survivors
- dread of separation

50s
- welfare of the families
- anxiety concerning drawn out death, personal suffering
- fear of being kept alive beyond hope of recovery

Figure 5. Focus of Concern for Those Facing "Early Death."

family members, and others to believe they should not speak honestly about the individual's illness and fears. They question whether the individual will be "able to take it," and wonder if it might not be "kinder" to protect the individual from the truth and the anxieties they know the truth must arouse.

A study reported in *Archiv für Psychiatrie und Nervenkrankheiten* notes that a number of investigations have reported from 66-88% of physicians as "discouraging total frankness" on the basis that a fatal prognosis "would be too great a strain for the patient and might lead to serious psychiatric problems." Other physicians "consider openness to be an important prerequisite of modern therapeutic methods, for these can be fully implemented only if the patients take an active part in decisions about their therapy."[1]

Yet many studies using a variety of methods have found that from 65-90% of the patients *are* in favor of being told the truth. One of the earliest and most consistent researchers in this area, Herman Feifel, "concluded that most seriously ill and terminally ill patients generally prefer honest, plain talk from physicians and family about the seriousness of their illness. They would like to voice their doubts, affirm their faith, and discuss what their impending separation means. They do not want their problems ignored or to receive false reassurance."[2]

Caring for Fears

This points us to a significant ministry for a caring Christian community. Brothers and sisters who care—whether doctors or nurses or pastors or simply friends from a congregation—can provide an atmosphere of warmth and acceptance, in which doubts and fears can be explored. We need not force our way past the present fears of the seriously ill to deal only with "spiritual realities." We can be God's agents of ministry to present needs as well.

It's important for us to recognize the spiritual roots of the temporal fears—and the spiritual resources to minister to them. The person with anxieties is raising basic questions about himself and his relationships. Self-doubt is reflected in such questions as "Can I stand the pain?" Uncertainty about personal worth is at the root of many other questions. "Who will care for my loved ones?" reflects both a desire to be important, and a fear for others' futures. To all such questions, the Christian brings a unique perspective.

You and I rightly doubt ourselves and our strength. But we have a God who has promised, "Never will I leave you; never will I forsake you" (Hebrews 13:5). Because God will live through the dying process with us, as well as receive us into glory, we can have confidence that He will strengthen us for every test.

You and I may doubt our value when we are no longer able to contribute and must be receivers rather than givers. Yet the Bible reveals that we have so much value to God that He gave His Son for us. "How will he not also, along with him, graciously give us all things?" (Romans 8:32).

It's right that we care about our loved ones. But God our Father cares for them, too. We may not be here to provide, but Jesus has taught us,

> Look at the birds of the air; they do not sow or reap or store away in barns, and yet your heavenly Father feeds them. Are you not much more valuable than they? Matthew 6:26

In God's promise of His presence; in God's affirmation of our individual worth and value; in God's commitment as a loving father to meet our basic needs, we find a firm foundation for trust. We are not insulated against the fears and anxieties associated with death and dying. But as we focus on the reality of God's love for us, and His commitment to us, God brings peace even in the turmoil.

There are, of course, times when verbal affirmations of spiritual realities may not be heard. But the continuing love of God's people can communicate those realities, even when doubt makes them seem unreal.

Jack experienced the reality of God's love even while rejecting Him. He experienced God's love through the caring of the deacon he'd angrily thrown out of his home. Let Ralph Neighbour continue the story.

"Later my deacon insisted I take him back, which I did *not* want to do. He said, 'I'm either going with or without you, and I think we'd both feel better if you went with me.' So we went. The wife refused to let us in. I begged her. I said, 'I know we made him angry before. But this is very, very important.'

"Finally she let us go in. He was in bed. He'd gotten considerably weaker over the last week.

"This deacon pulled out a little note pad and said, 'Jack, I know I offended you before. I humbly apologize. But I want you to know I've been working since then.

"'Your first problem is how will your wife and daughter have a place to live when she doesn't have any income. I checked in the neighborhood. You've owned this house for X number of years; I compute you have a minimum of X dollars in the house. We have a realtor in the church who's agreed to sell your house, and give your widow the real estate commission.

"'I guarantee you that a group of men along with me will make the payments for any months that might elapse till the house is sold. So stay here till you die, and if you'll permit me, we'll make your payments.

"'Then, right down the street, there's this large apartment house. I've contacted the owner. He's offered your wife a three-bedroom apartment for her and your daughter. When your house is sold, we'll move her over there. He will pay her $850 a month plus free utilities in return for which she can collect rents and supervise plumbing and electrical repair.

She'll be there till your daughter graduates from high school, and the income from your house should pay for her college.'

" 'The final thing is, I've gotten a team of young men from the church who've volunteered to pool their money and rent a U-Haul truck and move her, so it won't cost her a cent.'

" 'I want you to be able to die in peace, knowing that your wife and daughter are cared for. One thing I need is your permission to execute these plans for you after you've gone.'

"And Jack just cried like a baby."

Members of a caring community had communicated love —and met needs—in a way that went far beyond words.

When we think about the fears and the needs of those with life-threatening illnesses, we realize that often more than words is needed. A hug, a stroke, or simply holding hands, may communicate assurance of worth. God may use our listening as a person talks about his fears to help him reaffirm his faith. And at times we may be called on to act, and with deeds that match our words about God's Father-care, become the hands through which He provides the necessities of life.

As we do gather around others to care, the ultimate spiritual needs as well as present needs may be met. As fears about the present and the immediate future are relieved, the individual may be better able to hear the good news about a life that is eternal.

Shortly after the visit Ralph describes, Jack was taken to the VA hospital. His suffering was intense. He was so wrapped up in his pain that nothing else mattered, and he died without coming to Christ. But Jack's widow, touched by God's love as revealed in the caring community, did respond to the gospel message. For her, their love was a broad avenue leading to faith.

Reactions to Dying

While the fears we've just explored are common to all, individuals have a number of different ways of dealing with them. In her pioneering work, Dr. Elisabeth Kübler-Ross identified five "stages" of the dying process. As many (including Kübler-Ross) have pointed out, these are *not* one-two-three steps that each person takes during a terminal illness. In fact, it's best if we simply approach them as typical ways that persons may respond to the threat of approaching death. The tensions will be the same for everyone. How an individual responds to the tensions will differ.

While we want to understand something about these response patterns, and the clues to them which help us understand where a dying person is emotionally, it's important not to see them as "stages" or to suggest that one type of response is a "better" response than another. Instead, as we come to understand the responses we can better see how to comfort the individual *where he is*. And we can avoid judgmentalism when the individual most needs our support.

Denial. According to the *Facts of Death*, denial "is often used as a general term to cover any sort of behavior that allows a person to avoid facing reality, to evade a painful perception or to keep separate from it, or to escape confronting anything unpleasant."[3]

Many different responses under this broad definition are considered denial. For instance, studies of patients' perception of serious illnesses show that even those who have been clearly told the nature and the prognosis of their illness will typically grasp only a small part of the information, or even deny having been told anything. There is a very selective process in operation: much of what an individual may not want to hear simply is not heard or is forgotten. The news is too overwhelming for an individual to grasp and process all at once. As Roberts points out, "The individual needs time to recover from the psychological shock or threat of illness. The individual is only capable of absorbing a small portion of the threat. It is unrealistic to expect him to incorporate all of the shock at once." Thus the "function of denial is to reduce conflict and anxiety through alteration or distortion in perception of the threat."[4]

Denial takes many forms. It may involve failing to hear or understand a diagnosis. Or talk of a completely unrelated reason for being in the hospital. It may involve refusing to talk about anything related to death or illness. It may take the form of focusing on plans which are, at best, unrealistic, for a future "when I get well." Admission to a hospital may be interpreted as a sign of health rather than the seriousness of the illness: "they brought me in because they caught it early." Another form of denial may be religious: "God has healed me."

Denial is also selective in another sense. A person who is ill may adopt denial with some persons, and talk openly with others about the seriousness of his situation. This is often the case when a person is unsure how another is going to respond to honest interaction.

Often denial behavior is adopted with the doctor (if the patient perceives him as demanding recovery) or with family (if the patient is afraid the family won't be able to handle the truth). Cheerfulness and reassurance may even be perceived by the ill person as a sign that the visitor is afraid to face the truth, or unwilling to walk through the valley of the shadow with the sufferer.

Undoubtedly there are times when denial functions as one of God's gifts to give us time to cope. It may be a necessary defense for some people for part or much of the time of dying. Exaggerated denial, however, is usually harmful. A person may not take medication or follow a prescribed diet. He may build barriers between himself and loved ones so that the relational context is one of pretense (see page 17). Then denial can be unhealthy and even destructive. But in a supportive community it is hardly ever helpful—or necessary—to directly attack denial.

How do we relate to a person who's responded to life-threatening illness with some form of denial? First, be willing to relate where the person is. Express your love and concern and your acceptance. Some who practice denial will probe to see if we are accepting persons before risking exposure of fears or feelings of anger. If you're nonjudgmental about a person's denial, trust may grow to the place where he is free to explore some other response.

Individuals will usually give clues that they're ready to talk about death. They'll comment about "when I'm gone," and make little asides. If we ignore those asides we're signaling that we too are engaged in the game of pretense. If we rush in, we may go too far, too soon. Responding to the statement, but not pushing beyond it too rapidly, leaves the initiative with the individual. At the same time, it shows our willingness to deal with the realities that the person must, sooner or later, face.

In a little book entitled *Questions and Answers on Death and Dying*, Kübler-Ross gives this response to a person who asked, "How do you give a patient a clue that you will talk about death with him or her if he wants it?"

> I sit with him and talk about his illness, his pain, his hopes, and in a short time we are very often talking about our philosophies of life and death. Without any big preparations, we are in the midst of some real issues. Sometimes you can sit with a patient and ask him if he is willing to share with you what it's like to be so very ill. The patient will then talk about all the turmoil he has gone through and will perhaps add, "Sometimes I wonder if I would be better off to die." This gives you the opening to talk about what feelings, ideas, fears, and fantasies he has about death and dying.[5]

The point is simple. Warmth and caring, with a respect for what the individual wants to talk about or not talk about, helps create an atmosphere where denial is less necessary, and where other ways of responding to the threat of death can be tried.

Anger. As the threat of death is more and more clearly understood, fears and anxieties come. For most of us it's hard to recognize or to confess the anxiety. Instead it finds expression as envy, bitterness, and—commonly—as anger. We rebel against being cut off. There's nothing and no one to rebel against. Yet the feelings, fed by our frustration, are there. The unfairness of it all is overwhelming, and we strike out.

Anger may be expressed in irritation at conditions or persons around us. Anger may be expressed as conflict with family or medical personnel or friends. It may be directed against God, or against any nearby substitute. The flashes of anger, and the attacking behavior, may be embarrassing to the person who is ill. It is certainly painful to the person at whom attacks are directed. All too often bitterness and cutting remarks from a person we only want to help will stimulate our anger in return.

Of all typical responses to the threat of death, anger is the least socially acceptable. For Christians, who may be used to thinking of anger as sin, it's a very difficult reaction to respond to in a supportive way. Yet it hardly helps the patient to strike back at him, or to insist coldly that he get control of himself. We need instead to recognize the fact that it is fear and anxiety that are being expressed—that the angry person, too, needs the love and support of people who care.

How can we help the angry patient? First of all, listen. The anger may be focused on some irritant that should be corrected. Where there's a valid complaint, correcting it is a way of showing we care.

Second, listen with acceptance rather than condemnation. Don't draw back from the person, and don't strike out at him in reprisal. Realize that there is a deep and understandable need underlying the outbursts.

The problem here is that few people place themselves in the patient's position and wonder where
this anger might come from. Maybe we too would
be angry if all our life activities were interrupted so
prematurely; if all the buildings we started were to
go unfinished, to be completed by someone else; if
we had put some hard-earned money aside to enjoy
a few years of rest and enjoyment, for travel and
pursuing hobbies, only to be confronted with the
fact that "this is not for me."[6]

Realization leads to sympathy and understanding. With sympathy and understanding, with respect, and with the gift of a
little time, the person will be reassured that he is still valued.
Still worthwhile. Often listening and acceptance will help the
person work beyond his anger.

Psalm 73 reports the inner experience of a believer who
was moved to bitterness and frustrated anger by something
far less traumatic than the threat of death. Asaph was upset
when he saw the prosperity of the wicked, and compared his
own present troubles. He worked through his anger at God
and at the prosperous wicked, and was able to look back with
self-understanding.

> When my heart was grieved
>   and my spirit embittered,
> I was senseless and ignorant;
>   I was a brute beast before you.

What was it that brought him past the irrationality of his
anger? It was a restored awareness of God's continuing love,
even in his troubles. Finally he was able to affirm the great
reality which our sympathetic understanding and love can
help the terminally ill grasp as well:

> Yet I am always with you;
>   you hold me by my right hand.

You guide me with your counsel,
    and afterward you will take me into glory.
Whom have I in heaven but you?
    And being with you, I desire
    nothing on earth.
My flesh and my heart may fail,
    but God is the strength of my heart
    and my portion forever.
                                        Psalm 73:21-26

Bargaining. This response to the threat of death involves an implicit recognition that the end is approaching. But it seeks to put off the end...until. Perhaps it's a child's birthday that is set as a goal. "I just want to see Jane turn 18." Or "One last Thanksgiving with the family." At other times bargaining involves making promises to God or to oneself. "When I get well I'm going to spend more time with my family." Or "I'm sure that after this experience I'll be a much better witness."

There's little special response needed to bargaining, especially since many such bargains are made in secrecy. Perhaps it's best simply to see bargaining as a way of coming to grips with the reality of the illness. And to realize that often an individual *will* live until Jane's birthday, or until that last Thanksgiving. In cases like these bargaining is a way of fixing hope, of saying that in spite of the fact that I'm dying there's still something to live for.

For some, bargaining may be a part of the healing process. It's important, as we'll see later, to maintain hope. No one can ever say absolutely, whatever the illness, "You're going to die in six months." Too many remissions of cancer have occurred without medical explanation; too many miraculous recoveries have taken place. And hope is always an important element in getting well.

Depression. This is a fourth response to life threatening illness; one which is also completely understandable. We often feel sad when we leave a loved one to go on a trip, or when a child goes away for a vacation. How much more should we expect to feel the loss when everything and everyone that is familiar is going to be left behind? Weeping, despair, a sense of guilt, all these fit the category of depression and are completely normal.

Depression may be associated with the progress of a disease. The pain increases. The body weakens. It's necessary to be in the hospital. Life has changed because of financial pressures, because a job has had to be given up. The loss of the past and the coming loss of the future are likely to be experienced as an overwhelming grief.

How are we to help a person gripped by depression? It's important here that we comfort with our presence. Companionship, the quiet presence of those who care, may mean much more than words at such times.

It's also important to continue to give free and full acceptance to the feelings of the individual. Tears may not fit our notion of how a person should behave in the face of death. They do not fit the Greek concept of the brave death. They may not fit the idea of some of the Christian death as a victory or joyful exit into glory. But acceptance, letting the person know that he and his feelings are all right, is a way of freeing him to talk about the sense of loss. Kübler-Ross notes that "if he is allowed to express his sorrow he will find a final acceptance much easier, and he will be grateful to those who can sit with him during this state of depression without constantly telling him not to be sad."[7]

The comfort of a loving presence, and the comfort of prayer, is often most significant in times of depression.

Acceptance. The fifth response state suggested by Kübler-Ross as the final "stage" seems to involve neither envy or anger, and often to be beyond sorrow. Usually there are no strong feelings. It is in a sense a calm readiness to die.

At times the accepting response is hard for loved ones. It may be felt as withdrawal, or as a lack of love. But at this time too the presence of someone who cares, and is sensitive to the desire for peace, has meaning and does give comfort.

Dr. Johnson, with others, notes that acceptance often comes after the physical resources of the patient have been exhausted in fighting the disease. Thus it may well be a physically induced psychological state, a gift from God providing calm just before the end.

Not all terminally ill individuals will have a time of acceptance. Some will remain cheerful and alert; others will struggle to the last moment.

As with the other common types of response, acceptance is in itself neither right nor wrong, neither good nor bad. It is instead something that may exist and should be recognized by the caring community, and an appropriate kind of loving support provided.

Stages? It's important for us not, as we suggested at the beginning of this section, to view these "stages" as a necessary sequence of reactions through which each person ought to go for a "normal" terminal illness. As Simpson points out, "There are not five stages—there are three, fifteen, ninety-two, and five hundred. Though often seen [these five] are not —except probably for some variety of denial—*necessary* stages. They are very complex patterns of states of knowing and of emotional response, varying in whether they're last moments or weeks and firmly embedded in the person's personality and his approach to life."[8]

For those of us in the Christian community who seek to care for those with life-threatening illnesses, sensitivity to the typical responses described here is important. It's not that we are to diagnose or to categorize the people we minister to. It's simply that we need to realize that certain reactions are normal, to be expected, and that we can accept these reactions and continue to affirm the person. We are not called on to judge. We are called on to care, and to care in ways that individuals will be supported and helped. The real reason for understanding the responses then is not to monitor the feelings of the terminally ill or to evaluate their "progress," but to monitor our own feelings and responses to the things a dying person may say or do. If we have some idea of what to expect, and some idea of how to respond, our caring ministry will be much more effective.

"Ten Commandments" for Caring

Most of us will have times when we are with persons who have a life-threatening illness. Often our presence will be as representatives of a caring community of Christians, who love because God has first loved us. How can we show love in such a relationship? What practical guidelines will help? Dr. Paul Johnson gives these suggestions:

Always tell the truth. We need not tell all the truth at one time. And we need to speak the truth with love and sensitivity. But we should never belittle the problem, or minimize its seriousness for the sake of false reassurance. Integrity in this area will help to build a trust relationship in which ministry can take place.

Never set times. No one can tell how much time another person has to live. I've had many so-called "hopeless" cases where there was a reversal and recovery. No doctor can speak with certainty about the termination of life.

Listen with sensitivity. It's important to find out what the individual wants to talk about, and let him or her guide the conversation. It's also important to confess "I don't know" to questions about which we are not knowledgeable rather than provide misinformation.

Respond to needs. Listening for clues to the concerns that trouble the individual is important. So be alert to individuals for economic, psychological, family, and other needs, and minister to the needs revealed.

Never allow the person to feel abandoned. Often great care is taken medically to meet physical needs while emotional needs may be ignored. Calls, cards, flowers, visits — all are important. It's particularly important never to make a promise you can't later keep.

Make yourself available. It's important in a ministering relationship to be available at the person's request. Generally long visits are not helpful. Nor are more than two visitors at a time. But short, frequent visits are important.

Don't give medical advice. All too often well-meaning but ill-advised comments about clinics in this or that part of the country, treatments, or doctors, are made by visitors. Leave medical advice to the professional. If the person is uncertain or unhappy about his care, other doctors can and will be called in for consultation.

If necessary protect the person from himself. At times persons will attempt to treat themselves without telling their doctor, or will fail to take medication. Massive vitamin doses, fad diets, and many other forms of self-treatment may be tried. The person's doctor needs to know about such attempts at self-treatment, in case they might affect the treatment that has been prescribed.

Always hold out hope. However dark the situation, there is always something to be thankful for and something which can provide hope. It may simply be the hope of getting strong enough to go home for a time. But hope is very important, and always a reality.

Provide spiritual support. Relationship with God is vital for the dying person. Be open and honest about your own faith. Avoid heavy theological discussions and demands. But do share the simplicity of Jesus' love and presence in simple affirmation and prayer.

Developing Sensitivity

> Personal projects for individuals or study groups to help develop sensitivity for ministry with the terminally ill.

1.   Recall the five responses typically made by the terminally ill. Write them down. Describe their characteristics. Jot down how members of the caring community might helpfully respond in each situation.

2.   Which of Dr. Johnson's "Ten Commandments" seem most significant to you for your own personal relationship with those with life-threatening illnesses? How can you see it affecting what you say or do? (Be as specific as possible).

Chapter 3, Notes

1. P. Hartwich, "The Questions of Disclosing the Diagnosis to Terminally Ill Patients" in *Archiv für Psychiatrie und Nervenkrankheiten* 227 (1979): 23-32.

2. Glenn M. Vernon, *Sociology of Death* (New York: Ronal Press, 1970), p. 14.

3. Michael A. Simpson, *Facts of Death* (Englewood Cliffs, N.J.: Prentice-Hall, Inc., 1979), p. 37.

4. Sharon L. Roberts, *Behavioral Concepts and the Critically Ill Patient* (Englewood Cliffs, N.J.: Prentice-Hall, Inc., 1976), p. 183.

5. Elisabeth Kübler-Ross, *Questions and Answers on Death and Dying* (New York: Macmillan Co., 1974), p. 10.

6. Elisabeth Kübler-Ross, *On Death and Dying* (New York: Macmillan Co., 1969), p. 87.

7. Ibid.

8. Simpson, *Facts of Death*, p. 43.

Chapter 4

Those Who Care

"She dealt with the whole process of death long before the family was able to," Jim Bevis was saying. Jim is pastor of Brookvalley Church, in Atlanta, Georgia. The experience he was sharing helps us realize that life-threatening illness not only places a great strain on the ill person. It also can have a crushing impact on everyone around.

"She began to work through the various processes or stages of reaction long before the family was able to face the possibility, the reality, of her death. Once they did come around, and face the reality of it, there was a tendency to no longer treat her as a total person. For instance, before they were able to face the reality of the coming death, I never heard any conversation as to whether she was rational or not. But once they really faced up to the terminal nature of the illness, almost everything that she said was evaluated in that light. Is she rational? Does she really know what she's saying? How do we know that she really does know what she's saying?

"It was almost as though there was a loss of personhood. Now, these were very loving children. A very loving relationship. The changed relationship with their mother wasn't due to a lack of love, or anything close to that. But something seemed to switch in their minds once they were convinced she was terminal. It was almost as if she lost the right to live or to die. She lost the right to choose.

"Up until they faced the reality, she seemed to have respect and her right to choose. And I'd have to say it was true to some extent of the medical people as well."

When I talked with Jim about this experience, I asked him about the kinds of choices the family tried to take over. And I asked him about his role, as friend and pastor.

"One major battle was the choice of chemotherapy. She did not want it. It wasn't until I was able to convince the family that she had a right to make that choice, and until I was able to convince her that she was able to retain that right, that she agreed to enter chemotherapy.

"I was being poured on from both sides—the family wanting me to represent them, and she telling me things she wasn't telling them. We finally worked out a compromise. She agreed to enter into the chemotherapy, which the doctors and family felt would help relieve her pain, only if she could take her choice with her. We had that agreement, in the presence of all of them, that if at any point in time she told them to stop the treatment, it was her right."

Jim looks back and sees his role then as one of an advocate. An advocate because he seemed to be the only one who was hearing her and able to interpret what she was saying to the others. She was saying it to them. But somehow they would not listen to her.

Strangely, there had been no reason to doubt her ability to choose. She'd worked through the various reactions quickly, and approached the matter of death very systematically. She made her arrangements and talked through the questions of her will with the attorney long before the family faced the reality of her illness. She seemed almost to have a mental checklist of the things she needed to take care of. These, and internal problems like unforgiveness, she systematically faced and it wasn't until everything had been resolved that she died.

"Really, she wasn't the one who had the problems. It was her family."

The reaction of the family described by Jim isn't an unusual one. Everyone around a terminally ill person is affected by the dying process. There are pressures on the medical staff, on the family, on friends, and on ministers, which, though often unrecognized, have a dramatic impact on relationships with the terminally ill. All too often these unrecognized reactions, and the failure of those in the caring community to work through their own attitudes and needs, result in something that has been called "social death." There is a gradual, unintended, and yet deeply painful stripping away of the personhood of the terminally ill person. He is treated in many ways as if he was already dead, as respect given to him before the illness is gradually withdrawn.

In this chapter we want to survey some of the pressures on the medical personnel, the family, and those in the Christian community of brothers and sisters, which need to be recognized and dealt with to protect the personhood of and provide support for an individual living with a terminal illness.

Pressures on Medical Personnel

Kübler-Ross comments, "Early in my work with dying patients, I observed the desperate need of the hospital staff to deny the existence of terminally ill patients on their ward."[1] Many others have written on this topic, and pointed to a variety of reasons for this reaction. And it is a common reaction. Studies have shown that doctors avoid telling patients the facts about the seriousness of life-threatening illness.[2] Nursing staff tend to maintain pretense by reassurance, by withdrawal, or by treating the individual as a little child.[3]

Part of the reaction comes from the individual's natural discomfort with death. Professional people are no more immune from discomfort in a relationship with a terminally ill person than anyone else. But there is also pressure from the values instilled in medical training.

> At this stage of training, death is viewed as the enemy, the opponent, something waiting to snatch away the patient. "The whole idea of medical training," said one physician, "is to teach doctors how to avoid death at almost any cost." So the battle lines are drawn, with death lurking in the shadows in mortal conflict with the physician, attired appropriately in white. At stake is not only the patient's life, but also the clinician's reputation and self-respect."[4]

James Knight writes of "The Physician's Ministry to the Dying" and points out that "the care of terminal patients arouses some of the most pervasive fears in man—extinction, victimization, helplessness, abandonment, disfigurement, and above all, loss of self-esteem. The physician who treats such patients is subject to these fears."

But there is even more. The physician is bound to the dying patient, and "must face his own sense of failure, guilt, and intimations of personal mortality. In such a situation, there is a tendency to withdraw from the dying."[5]

All these concerns of medical personnel—the commitment to prolong life, the personal stake in recovery, the hesitancy to talk openly about the seriousness of diseases— along with other unusual behavior (such as the spiriting of bodies off hospital wards in disguised carts, and anger in some nurses about a dying patient "taking up space"), point to the fact that medical professionals are often unready to deal with the terminally ill. The "stages" of denial, anger, and the rest experienced by the dying person have also been observed in medical staff caring for such patients.

In the process of dealing with their own feelings and needs, medical personnel may rob the patient of what he or she most fears to lose...a sense of personal significance and worth. Stripped of respect, treated as a child, told only half-truths, the dying person may pass to a strange state of social death before physical death comes.

What can medical personnel do to be supportive and helpful? First of all, realize that the individual's life is his as long as it remains and treat him with respect. Thus a high degree of honesty and integrity are needed, for only then will the individual be treated as a whole person. Along with this basic requirement, Ruth A. Ansel suggests several ways in which medical people can serve as advocates for the rights of the dying person.[6]

Be available to the dying person. This includes readiness to answer questions honestly, to listen sensitively, and to talk about feelings as well as medical matters. The basic emphasis is to develop a personal relationship rather than dealing with the physical body technologically.

Make provision for significant others to be with the dying person. This at times will involve modification of hospital visitation policies, which are usually set for the convenience of the institution rather than the needs of the patients. It also may involve serving, as Jim Bevis did, as an advocate with the family, helping them understand the patient's rights and wishes.

Make an effort to surround the dying person with those things that are familiar, habitual, or of value to him. Medical care facilities are often impersonal, sterile places. The patient, already threatened by his illness, is often stripped of the familiar things which help him or her feel at home. As much as possible, normal clothing, items from home, and favorite foods should be made available. Here again a relaxation of typical hospital rules can provide significant support for and ministry to the individual.

There's a growing medical literature on death and dying, and there is greater sensitivity today by medical personnel to the needs of the terminally ill. But we should not be surprised if we encounter insensitivity. Death and dying are difficult for professional people as well as for the rest of us. But if we do find insensitivity to the needs of the terminally ill, it's important for us, as members of a caring community, to be an advocate for the patient with the staff.

Pressures on the Family

Even when a deep bond of love links members of the family, there's the likelihood that family members may intensify the pain of dying. The woman described by Jim Bevis was actually forced to defend herself and her right to choose against those who cared most for her.

Not that the family should be blamed. They too are going through a painful time. Yet there are many ways that family members can make dying more difficult. Some will try to maintain a false front of cheerfulness, never letting the individual express or share his feelings. Others will insist that the individual is getting better, or talk only about future plans and how much the dying person is needed, so that a burden of guilt is added to the patient's strain.

We need to realize that the family is going through a painful time. That they need help to understand their feelings and reactions. That they need guidance to know how to best support the dying person.

A family or family members will often work through the Kübler-Ross "stages" also. Usually they will not reach a "stage" at the same time as the dying person. Thus it's not unusual for family members to deny the seriousness of an illness long after the person himself has accepted it. Anger—at God, and at others—is common. Normally there is even resentment directed toward the dying person, for deserting

them, for being too demanding, etc. Depression and bargaining aren't unusual. At times the family accepts the death well
before it comes. They grieve until grief is past, and then may
even become annoyed when the person does not die when
they are ready.

None of this is done consciously or maliciously. The tensions of the terminal situation create pressures in which such
feelings are a normal experience. Like the feelings of the ill
person, the family's reactions need to be recognized and
worked through, and supportive relationships provided.

Ministry to Family Members Checklist

The family is aware of the nature, treatment, and
prognosis of the disease .... ☐

The family understands the likely reactions of
the patient to terminal illness .... ☐

The family members have supportive relationships with others to whom they can talk and express their feelings and needs .... ☐

Transportation, baby-sitting, and other needed
help are provided to allow family members to
visit .... ☐

Family members have been provided with "time
off" for recreation, rest or just time to be on their
own .... ☐

Spiritual counsel is available to the family as
well as to the dying person .... ☐

The need to give the dying person as much control as possible over himself and his routines is
understood .... ☐

There are relationships in which grief can be
freely expressed, and these expressions are
accepted .... ☐

Figure 6. Ministry to Family Members Checklist.

The family checklist (Figure 6) gives us a framework to
explore the special needs of the family, and points to ways

that members of the caring community can support the family as well as minister to the dying person.

Let's work through the checklist, and see some of the ways in which a caring community can help with pressures on families.

Is the family aware? We suggested earlier that it's best to work toward a context of open awareness between the terminally ill individual and medical people. This means that there is no need for pretense on either side: each recognizes the seriousness of the illness and can deal with realities, yet each retains hope. This is important for families as well. Too often family members perceive denial in the way doctors deal with their loved one, and withhold information or pretend as if they also were to keep "medical secrets." As we've seen, we can expect some denial from the family as well as from the doctors and the dying person. Denial isn't always wrong; it may be helpful in coping—for a time. But if the family and patient are to deal constructively with a life-threatening illness, and to develop and maintain a relationship of openness in which support can be given and received, an approach to openness does need to be made.

Does the family understand likely reactions? It's important for the family members to understand the fears outlined in the last chapter, and the possible reactions of the individual. Often family members turn inward, working through their own feelings and needs, and are unable to be sensitive to their dying loved one. Some understanding of feelings and typical reactions will help the family with their own feelings, and help them be more sensitive to the ill person.

Has the family adapted to changes in responsibilities? In every family system different members have different roles and responsibilities. One member takes care of business and finances. Another deals with meals and cleaning. One may take care of repairs and purchases for upkeep of the house.

Another may know the children's schedules and needs for rides.

A terminal illness to either parent, or to one of the children in the family, may mean radical changes in responsibilities. Even such simple things as bill paying and balancing the checkbook may be difficult if one has never needed to do it. Thus ministry to the family may mean helping a person carry out responsibilities he or she is completely unprepared for. Someone to pick up the slack, or to show a family member how, can be a significant help.

Are there supportive relationships? We've mentioned the desirability of the terminally ill person having a relationship with someone or with several persons in which he is free to share his feelings and doubts and fears. Supportive listening, affirmation and acceptance, are very important in times of tension.

At times we forget that family members may well be facing the same kinds of fears and feelings as the ill person. At times the personal resources of family members will be exhausted in trying to deal with their own feelings, so they have little left to give in support of the dying person. The caring community needs to gather around the family members as well, to maintain relationships in which sharing of the family members' feelings can take place, and support be provided.

Is transportation, etc., available? Sometimes the little things seem hardest to bear. And often it's the little things that a caring community can most easily provide. Is there transportation? Will someone be home when the children return from school? Are baby sitters available for the evening? In the Colorado situation mentioned in chapter one, members of the congregation fed pets and watered plants. They came in and cleaned the home and brought hot meals. One brother insisted the husband whose wife was dying play tennis with him regularly. The whole congregation gathered around in prayer, and the deep concern of the fellowship as well as the little things they did to meet daily needs provided essential support.

Is provision made for "time off"? It's important for the well-being of the family members that they do not become "trapped" by the dying, or "feel obligated to live constantly with the illness, seldom leaving the bedside, and feeling guilty if they occasionally think of laughing or amusing themselves, or continuing their normal lives."[7]

The feeling of being trapped is common. It's natural to even feel angry or exploited at times if a loved one requires intense time and care. These feelings often create guilt: the family member feels ashamed and condemns himself. Yet these reactions are normal, just as are the reactions of the dying person to his situation. Provision of "time off," of the opportunity to rest and recuperate or engage in a favorite activity, is important to reduce the pressure on families. Providing someone to take on the care duties as well as being friends with whom one can talk and share feelings is an important ministry of the caring community to the family.

Is spiritual counsel available? When members of the Christian community gather around to support a family, God is present in His family. Our prayers, our words of affirmation, are all important to family members. As with the dying person, preaching or deep theological discussion is seldom appropriate. But a simple faith, and simple reminders of God's continuing love and care, are always meaningful.

It is not surprising that doubt is often part of the dying process for the person and his family. "Why would God do this?" is a question all ask, and a question which ultimately has no answer. The psalmists not only felt doubts, but they expressed them. And in nearly all cases, the progress of the psalm shows the individual coming at last to faith's affirmation of God's love and goodness.

This is just as true for us today. God *is* with us. And as we continue with the community of faith to affirm His goodness, all involved in the trauma of dying will find comfort and strength in His love.

Is the need to respect the dying person understood? Jim Bevis's story points up the tendency to rob the dying person of his freedom to choose, and of his self-respect. Family members will often do this out of love. Like the family in Jim's story they accept the imminence of death — and their attitude toward the individual may change.

There are other ways of stripping the dying person of his self-respect. A wife talks only of how much she needs the dying husband, and reminds him of his promise to fix the porch. The wife is not only practicing denial, she is very likely producing guilt. She is projecting her needs, and her sense of desertion, on her husband. In essence, she is telling him that he cannot die. Her needs, not his, are understandably expressed, but expressed in such a way that his burden is increased, as guilt for deserting his dependents is added to his load.

It may be that such statements are meant to cheer. But when they fail to show sensitivity to the individual's needs and his wishes, they can be harmful to both parties.

Other ways of stripping control from a patient involve refusal to talk over daily events or problems of the home. This too may be experienced as a social death — as being cut off from all that was important; as being unneeded or unwanted.

Basically, our goal is to involve the dying person in decision making to the extent that he wants to be involved. By giving him as much control over things that relate directly to his care or situation (what he eats, what he wears, what treatments he accepts or rejects, what things he wants to talk about and share), we protect his sense of significance and show him the respect due to a responsible and valuable human being.

Are expressions of grief accepted? Many have noted that grieving will, and should, begin before death in the case of a relatively lengthy terminal illness. Anticipatory grief can be expressed to brothers and sisters in the Christian community, and the grief accepted and shared. Family and patient may even be able to grieve together. The main point here is that grief should not be rejected or judged. "Bearing up bravely" isn't something we can require of family any more than we require it of the dying person. No one is completely comfortable with grief. But when the times of grieving come, we want to comfort by being able to weep with our hurting friends.

In examining the pressures on the family, and in suggesting a checklist for ministry to the family, we've said implicitly and explicitly that the family of the dying person is also in need of ministry by the caring Christian community. There are also one or two specific questions about death and the family that need attention. Particularly, should the person with terminal illness die at home—or in the hospital?

This is a question that has no general answer. Some families are well-adjusted, with healthy relationships between the members and good communication. Home has been a place of warmth and the focus of the individual's life. In such a situation, the seriously ill person will most likely want to be at home. And the family members will want him there. When there is the desire to be at home, it's undoubtedly best to provide home care rather than hospital care.

But not all families are warm and healthy. In many there are already strained relationships, broken communication lines, and relationships which are more of a burden than a support under the strain of the terminal illness. In such cases being at home may be more difficult for the individual and the family as the illness worsens than being in a hospital or other care facility.

The determining factor in any situation should not be our theory of "what's best for a terminal patient." Instead the determining factor should be the wishes of the person and the family. We should realize that in every family there will be a nèed to receive outside support and help. That support can come from the loving larger family of fellow believers, whose love is living evidence that God does care, and thus is a great gift from the Lord to His people.

Pressures on the Community

To this point we've written as if only the individual, the medical personnel, and the family needed help. Almost as if the Christian community—brothers and sisters who gather around to care—did not. This is not true. In fact, none of us is comfortable in the face of death. Often Christians draw back in discomfort, rather than draw near. Fear and hostility toward death often block the sympathetic and understanding ministry which we all need from the community of faith.

While part of our discomfort is rooted in not knowing what to say or what to do that will help, part is also linked to the Christian's uncertainty about death. Few of us have thought seriously of our own death. Fewer still have ever uttered the psalmist's prayer,

> Show me, O LORD, my life's end
>   and the number of my days;
>   let me know how fleeting is my life.
> Psalm 39:4

Facing our frailty, and affirming with the whole community of faith across the ages that both life and death can be entrusted to a faithful God, is a valuable spiritual exercise for all of God's people.

As we saw in the first chapter, there have been definite changes in the patterns of dying in modern society. A shift in the causes of death has led to a longer time span for dying. Our lengthened lives mean that increasingly it is the older person who faces death. Many of us are insulated from death through decades of our lives. The majority of people in our country die in some kind of health care facility, not at home.

We Christians, like others in our society, are not really familiar with death and dying as a part of normal life.

We can add to these the fact that a person working through the feelings associated with life-threatening illnesses is not normally attractive. The emotions are too painful; the expression of inner anguish too uncomfortable. Such feelings make us want to draw back. We can sense the dark uncomfortableness of relationships with a dying person by reading Psalm 88, where the psalmist expresses many of the reactions that we've seen are common during a terminal illness.

> O LORD, the God who saves me,
>   day and night I cry out before you.
> May my prayer come before you;
>   turn your ear to my cry.
>
> For my soul is full of trouble
>   and my life draws near the grave.
> I am counted among those who go down to the pit;
>   I am like a man without strength.
> I am set apart with the dead,
>   like the slain who lie in the grave,
> whom you remember no more,
>   who are cut off from your care.
>
> You have put me in the lowest pit,
>   in the darkest depths.
> Your wrath lies heavily upon me;
>   you have overwhelmed me with all your waves.
> You have taken from me my closest friends
>   and have made me repulsive to them.
> I am confined and cannot escape;
>   my eyes are dim with grief.
>
> I call to you, O LORD, every day;
>   I spread out my hands to you.
> Do you show your wonders to the dead?
>   Do those who are dead rise up and praise you?

Is your love declared in the grave,
  your faithfulness in Destruction?
Are your wonders known in the place of darkness,
  or your righteous deeds in the land of oblivion?

But I cry to you for help, O LORD;
  in the morning my prayer comes before you.
Why, O LORD, do you reject me
  and hide your face from me?

From my youth I have been afflicted and close to
    death;
  I have suffered your terrors and am in despair.
Your wrath has swept over me;
  your terrors have destroyed me.
All day long they surround me like a flood;
  they have completely engulfed me.
You have taken my companions and loved ones
    from me;
  the darkness is my closest friend.

In this psalm we read most of the reactions and emotions of a person living under the threat of death. There is social death ("I am set apart with the dead") and abandonment ("you have taken from me my closest friends and have made me repulsive to them"). There is a dark sense of guilt ("your wrath lies heavily upon me") and fear ("I have suffered your terrors... your terrors have destroyed me"). There is anger ("from my youth I have been afflicted") and there is despair ("my eyes are dim with grief...[I] am in despair"). There is bargaining ("do those who are dead rise up and praise you?") and depression ("the darkness is my closest friend").

As we read this psalm, each of us instinctively draws back. There's nothing beautiful, nothing attractive, nothing desirable here. We turn away from this dark picture, and turn quickly to find a psalm more uplifting or comforting.

It's no wonder that members of the Christian community are not attracted to a death and dying ministry. In terms of personal discomfort, and personal cost, the price of such a ministry is high. It's much easier to expect the minister (who is the "professional" in spiritual care) and the family members (who are bound to the dying person by blood) to meet the great needs that exist. Pressures on brothers and sisters in the wider family are just as real and just as great as those on the persons who *must* spend time with the dying individual. The difference is that the members of the wider community are not compelled by duty or necessity to respond.

What is so encouraging, however, is to realize that as those near the individual *do* respond, they can be God's messengers of love and support. Doctors who are sensitive to the personal and spiritual needs of the patient as well as to his physical condition can minister significantly. Nurses who understand a patient's responses can provide support. Brothers and sisters from the caring community, along with family, can gather around to care and to communicate God's presence to the man or woman trudging through the valley of the shadow of death.

By our presence and care we can rescue the individual from social death, so he no longer feels "I am set apart with the dead" before physical death comes. We can be sure that he or she never feels "you have taken from me my closest friends and have made me repulsive to them." We can affirm his continuing value to us as a person. We can listen as he shares feelings of guilt and fear and talks out his anger. Together we can affirm a love of God which frees us from guilt through the message of forgiveness in Christ; that reduces our fear by affirmation of God's unchanging commitment of love.

The caring community, gathering around as a family to support the dying person, can make a significant difference in the experience of death.

We've already seen illustrations of the differences that the support of the caring community can make. In Colorado, a congregation gathered around Cathy, supporting her and her family in a myriad of simple and practical ways. She was a Christian. Up to that point, her husband had not responded to the Gospel. Today he is a believer, and a part of the fellowship whose love he experienced.

In Houston, a brother worked actively to meet some very basic needs of dying Jack. He and the others in that caring community did relieve the anguish of a dying man, and their active love guided Jack's wife to faith, and membership in that same Christian community.

In Atlanta, a sensitive pastor was able to be an advocate for both a dying woman and her family, and through his ministry help each through the pain and misunderstandings caused by a terminal illness.

In each of these situations, and in thousands and thousands of others, the response of a caring community of Christians has made a significant difference.

Expectations

We hope it's clear we're not suggesting that the ministry of a caring community can transform dying into a pleasant, or even a victorious, experience. In the *Journal of Health Politics, Policy and Law*, Dr. Thomas Helper writes appropriately of the "unmistakable arrogance in those who would lay the natural and functional anxiety about dying to rest, in the belief that death is a problem to be solved if only it were talked about openly, as if it were halitosis or venereal disease." As he suggests, "death and dying are not these kinds of problems. To think of them in such terms is not merely false and misleading. Equally important, it trivializes and sentimentalizes consideration of life's supremely profound mystery."[8]

In exploring death and the caring community, we do not want to trivialize death or dying. Or to suggest "solutions" to problems for which human beings, captive in the bonds of mortality, have no answers.

What we do want to suggest is that God, who does not insulate His people from tragedy, commits Himself to be with us in times of trial. He strengthens us, and works out His own mysterious good through every circumstance. We are compelled, by the biblical revelation of how God works in our lives to provide strength and comfort, to realize that the Church, as the family of God, is one major avenue for provision of support. Gathering around to care for those among us who live in death's shadow is a significant ministry. It is a living expression of God's presence and His love.

In our exploration to this point we have attempted to survey the serious needs that emerge in a terminal situation. We've suggested that with understanding, helpful and supportive responses can be made. In the chapters that follow we want to outline more completely ways that members of the Christian community can respond to such needs, and provide the caring and support which are so important to everyone involved.

Developing Sensitivity

> Personal projects for individuals or study groups to help develop sensitivity for ministry with the terminally ill.

1.   Imagine that you have been stricken with a life-threatening illness. What changes might your illness make in your family's life style? How would you expect each family member to react? What kinds of support from a caring community would be most helpful, or most needed by them?

2.   Read Psalm 88 several times. How do the psalmist's words make you feel? Imagine yourself sitting with the psalmist as he expresses these feelings. How might you respond to him? What could you say or do that would be most supportive, and best communicate the presence of God to him?

Chapter 4, Notes

1. Elisabeth Kübler-Ross, *On Death and Dying* (New York: Macmillan Co., 1969), p. 249.

2. Michael A. Simpson, *Facts of Death* (Englewood Cliffs, N.J.: Prentice-Hall, Inc., 1979), p. 93.

3. Ibid.

4. Robert H. Coombs and Pauline S. Powers, "Socialization for Death," in *Toward a Sociology of Death and Dying*, ed. Lyn H. Lofland (Beverly Hills, Ca.: Sage Publications, 1976), p. 25.

5. James Knight, quoted in Simpson, *Facts of Death*, p. 43.

6. Ruth A. Ansel, "If You Were Dying," in *The Dying Patient: A Supportive Approach*, ed. Rita E. Caughill (Boston: Little, Brown and Co., 1976), pp. 58-62.

7. Kübler-Ross, *On Death and Dying*, p. 218.

8. Dr. Thomas Helper, editorial in *Journal of Health, Politics, Policy and Law*, 12, no. 3 (Fall 1979).

Chapter 5

Opportunities to Care

*T*hus far in our exploration of the impact of life-threatening illness, we've met several individuals who have been ministered to significantly by a caring community of Christians. In this chapter we want you to meet a number of other individuals. Some of them have passed the crisis in their struggle with death. Others know that their death is only a few days or weeks or months away. As you read their words, and listen in on their thoughts, listen with sensitivity. Ask, how might I or others support this individual? How do his or her words reveal opportunities for significant ministry by members of Christ's own caring community?

Dora

Dora has been Paul Johnson's patient for a number of years. When she was forty-nine she had breast cancer, and a radical mastectomy. In an interview with Paul Johnson she remembers that time, now some seven years in her past.

Whether I had the cancer or Phil had had the cancer, I don't think the impact could have been any different. Our relationship has always been close. We were married when we were 18, 19-years old, and we've always had an extra strong relationship.

I went to another doctor first—a Doctor Griffins, I think. He told me that I was going to die, and to come back when I started hurting. He wouldn't even order the chemotherapy that you did. Now that was a real trauma for me— bigger than the mastectomy.

I remember coming out after an X-ray scan, and seeing him standing in the hall. I said to my friend who'd brought me to the hospital, "That doctor told me I am going to die. He said I have cancer in my spine and brain, but I'm not going to tell Phil." My friend told me I had to. So I remember coming home, and Phil said, "There's something wrong. Tell me what it is."

So I took the advice of my neighbor, and Phil and I just talked. With no dinner, no nothing, we just talked into the wee hours of the morning. We talked about the past, and about how, with the kids about to be gone, now was the time we were looking forward to. And we wondered why it was being taken away from us. I don't think there was ever a time we were so close as those hours.

We cried. We laughed about funny jokes. I don't remember bringing God into it at all. We didn't blame Him. But in the nights during that year, you know how you can't sleep and you prowl around the house by yourself, and you say, "Why?" And you think of the things maybe you've done that He doesn't agree with. Or maybe you've taken this terrific life that you have for granted. You know, you think crazy things. You're always looking for an answer, and it isn't something you can ask anyone.

I couldn't go to Phil and say, "Why did God do this to me?" It would only get him upset, and he doesn't have the answer. I don't know if God brings these things or not. But I can't say God puts us through them. I did get upset and angry and sometimes screamed at God. But it was just a reaction, because I couldn't accept being separated from Phil now.

Really, I know God's not the kind of Person to do something that bad.

Anyway, when I left the hospital and left the doctor's office, I had the feeling that the doctor was angry at me. I don't know why. He made me feel like I was taking his time and he was angry with me. Actually, he was the only medical person who treated me cold like that. And later I came to you. Then I felt you'd take care of me. I had chemotherapy, and at the hospital they were very warm, and I had my operations.

My operations covered three years. First there was a lump in one arm. Then the next year I had a hysterectomy. Then the next year it was a mastectomy.

I knew Phil was terribly worried when I got cancer, and I hated to see the hurt in his face. I also felt that with the last operation I'd spoiled something for him. I wasn't afraid he'd not like me, but I was afraid I'd ruined something important for him. After I had my breast removed, I wouldn't look at myself for weeks. But it didn't bother him any, and he was constantly reassuring me.

I have a friend in that situation now, and her husband is putting her down. And I can't imagine that.

Nobody I knew talked much with me about God. But when I got the news the cancer was gone, it was as if I pushed open a door and saw this tremendous light. I don't know, it was almost as if God had His arms around me. That Jesus had made me well. I don't know if I could have accepted talking with anyone at the time I had my surgery. You're trying to sort out so many things, and are so confused. I just wanted to do that myself.

Now my brother had cancer, too, and some minister came and told him if he prayed with him he'd be all right. My brother had never been a religious man, but had gone in a different direction.

But he did pray with him, and he followed this man all over the country. I had to go with him, because he had blood cancer. Finally when he was in the hospital for the last time, they told him he had to go off to this healing meeting. I wouldn't let him. And they told me if my brother died it would be my fault, because I didn't have enough faith.

I believe. But I couldn't believe that. But what did make me happy was that in this whole thing my brother did find Jesus, and he died content. So even that gave him a peace no medicine could give.

Actually, looking back, I'm almost thankful I had to go through my own experience with cancer. It's made me so much richer in so many ways, and opened my eyes to the things that I have. So I appreciate life more. I think it's enriched Phil's life, too. It's made us so much more aware of what we have together.

Avis

Avis is a nurse, a night supervisor of a large hospital, who has the same life-threatening kind of cancer that struck Paul Johnson. Like Paul, Avis is a Christian. And her faith did make a difference. She tells about the two years since her diagnosis.

I'm just now beginning to be able to discuss my problem. I feel like I'm over the worst. Some people I know have tried to get me to talk a lot about it, but I couldn't. It was just too soon. There has to be a healing first, emotional and psychological. When it happens to you, it's a kick in the head, and until you get over that you're just in a deep hole.

You can reach out for other people, but you gotta do it yourself. It's like an alcoholic. You have to admit to yourself that you've got this, and you're going to have to live with it, and the future is up to you.

It was right before Christmas time when I came to you with this lump. I think I knew even before anyone told me. The other doctor wouldn't come out and say it, but I knew inside. Then when I came to you I knew I had big trouble.

My first reaction was to try to blank it out. Even though I really knew it, I just wasn't going to think about it. I wasn't panicky; I was just numb.

As a nurse I'm used to crisis and stress. And I think I kept thinking about it as if it was happening to somebody else, not me. Of course, now when I see someone going to surgery for a biopsy or possible radical mastectomy, I can appreciate a lot more how they feel. But I was just numb, and kept on functioning.

Actually, everything had been going good with me. Good job, good money, good house. Oh, there were problems, but nothing big. And then this happens. It brought the realization of need for God, right now. And I knew He was there, and He was going to help.

I tried to think, Now, why should this be happening to me? But I really didn't blame God. I've heard a lot of people blame God, or think they're being punished. But I felt right away the need for God to be real close; I just wanted Him right here. It was the only thing that really helped me at the time.

Even so, I had some down periods. My mother couldn't accept my sickness. So Mary Jane, a friend of mine, gave me the most help. She talked to me sensibly. She wasn't a Christian then, but since she's been baptized. I think my sickness helped her realize she needed God, too.

I've thought about it a lot, and I think God was trying to teach me something, too. Before, I used to buy a lot of things I didn't need. Things meant a lot to me. But now they really don't. My priorities have changed, and I plan things differently for the future.

That's what hit me right off the bat. All my plans are going to go right down the tube. This didn't seem fair to me. You know, I'd just sold my house and bought another one to take care of my mother, and here I wasn't going to be there to take care of her. It bothered me a lot, wondering what was going to happen.

Then finally it dawned on me. She's going to get along without me, just like before. And from then on I learned to relax. I'm not afraid of dying now. Death doesn't bother me. It's the way I die that bothers me. That worries me more than anything. I don't want to be just kept alive.

Oh, I've had some low points. I remember, I was afraid to think almost. My liver studies were way off, and they were checking everything out before I started chemotherapy. I knew how bad it would be if it was in my liver, and I really felt terrible. But my liver scan was negative. And all I said on the phone was, "Thank God," and then I cried for two hours. It was such a relief.

Even so, at first I felt alone. Not ostracized, but I felt that I was sort of special in a group. That people acted differently toward me. The ones I knew who were Christians seemed more comfortable, and they talked about it with me. But the rest of them just said "How are you?" and "that's great" and left. The Christians really cared, and I could feel that.

I had a lot of people come up to me to help. I was just dumbfounded. There were some people in Australia, and they were going to pray for me. Somebody knew someone in Chicago, and they were going to pray. There was the little girl next door. She prayed for me every night for weeks. And it just amazed me, that all these people would come up and say they're praying. It really felt warm.

A lot of friends talked to my mother, not to me. But even they sent cards and I knew they cared.

When this first happened to me, I didn't give myself a year. I thought, well, it's going to happen. So I got everything ready, and told my brother what to do, and everything. It really scared him. But I don't worry about what's going to happen any more. I know I can cope with it.

Clyde

Clyde is a retired electrician and plant engineer. He and his wife had been married for nearly fifty years when he was discovered to have a cancer that led to major surgery and a permanent colostomy.

When I first learned about it, I didn't know what to do: whether to carry on and let it go, or to go into the hospital for treatment. I'm not much for hospitals. But I realized it was bad. It was quite a trauma, mostly because I didn't want to leave my wife all by herself.

My disease was a cancer of the colon, and I had to have very major surgery. What I feared was being laid up, and not knowing how I'd come out of it.

I'd never been around anyone who had this thing. When I came home with the diagnosis, my wife told me there was nothing I could do but trust my surgeon and do what he asked. And then she said, "Whatever happens, we'll see it through together." So we just kept talking and talking, and sometimes I'd cry a bit. The way they were going to carve me up, you know, was going to, well....

Anyway, we could talk it out, like we always have. And we told all our nieces and nephews, who've always been very close to us. We didn't have any children. And they were all shook up about this thing.

After the operation happened and I came home, I realized it was a permanent thing. Then I did get down pretty low. I probably would have done something [to myself] then, if it had been available. What helped most was just talking to her, crying a little. And she'd say, "You say you love me, but doing something like that would be selfish." But when I got home and realized I had to take care of it myself, that was another thing. Now I'm getting along fine, but then, well....

My wife prayed a lot. At first she prayed to make me well and bring me home. Then she got to thinking, "That's selfish." Then she prayed for strength and courage to see this through. She didn't want me to come home if I was going to be unhappy or hurting. So she prayed for courage and strength. And her praying made her calmer, and she was my source of strength.

Pat

Pat, a supervising nurse in a large hospital, has worked for many years with the life-threatened. When Paul Johnson interviewed Pat he asked her for her observation of their most pressing needs—and what has been of greatest help.

Normally the most immediate need of acute patients (those in danger of immediate traumatic death) is coping with the panic that results from pain or shortness of breath. For these patients, control of the pain is the first concern. If the pain isn't relieved, they never get beyond that pressing, immediate need.

But then when pain is taken care of, the next issue is loss of control. The patients I've observed who suffer the most are those who have no one or nothing to turn to; no faith that the situation is somehow under control.

Most who face life-threatening illnesses feel their own control of their lives and future slipping away. Even though they have support from their families, or others, they really have no one to whom they can release control of their lives. But people with life-threatening illnesses need to turn to someone who has control. And they suffer a great deal until they come to that point. Those who don't believe in God suffer immense anxiety, and even those who do believe suffer until they begin to focus on the right things.

In my experience, when people in an acute setting have their pain relieved, they move right away to things they've got to settle, like who's going to take care of the kids, or how they're going to pay the bills, and so on. The focus is on *things.*

But people in a chronic setting (with a disease in which a longer, drawn out dying process can be expected) are much

different. They have more time to talk and think. These people have a great need for that sense of control when they're
first told, and then later as physical deterioration from the
disease becomes more pronounced. Patients in this setting
tend to talk about guilt. They think back over their lives, and
fasten on personal failures. They feel the sickness is somehow
their fault, and they'll talk about how they used to go to
church but stopped, or about a divorce, or about how they
didn't raise their children properly. They have a tendency not
to fasten on immediate things, but on the past and on reasons
why their sickness might have happened. These people tend
to feel that their present is retaliation, because they didn't do
what they should have during their lives.

Usually with patients who I sense are overwhelmed, I
simply say, "Are you afraid?" And most of them cry—men
and women. Tears come to their eyes. I ask that question
after a patient sort of knows me. They cry because it's such a
relief to be able to talk about their doubts and fears.

For those who haven't been religious before, it's difficult
to help them relate to giving their life over to someone. So if
they do not have faith, it's difficult at that time. They can
learn it, and really do need to, but it's so difficult for them
because they don't understand.

Yet they are willing to give their life over to anyone they
can trust, and when they do turn it over to God, they seem
much more peaceful.

Earl

*Earl is a medical doctor. He's a very quiet man who,
when Paul Johnson interviewed him, had less than a month
to live. Throughout his illness, Paul had been impressed at
Earl's calm and apparent peace as his life came swiftly to an
end. Here's a transcript of a conversation the two had which
illustrates in several ways the value of Pat's comments
(above) on turning over control in a life-threatening
situation.*

Paul: Earl, you developed a malignancy, primarily of the pancreas, wasn't it?

Earl: Liver.

Paul: Liver? Oh, really.

Earl: Liver primarily.

Paul: Now, under chemotherapy, you're going through the same stages I went through. The thing that bothered me, Earl, is I also lost my eyelashes.

Earl: Is that right? I've been surprised that mine haven't...

Paul: It really bothered me. I think it bothered me more than the hair on my head. I lost everything. But, anyway, thanks for coming in to contribute to this book that we hope will help somebody else.

   The reason we're doing it is that most seminars on dying leave out what I think is the most important aspect.

Earl: Yeah.

Paul: I just want to, sort of, get some information from you, while you're going through it. And it's tough when you're going through it. How do you keep going?

Earl: Well, I knew right from the beginning it was an incurable situation. I got the diagnosis on Christmas Eve...(Earl's voice breaks)

Paul: Did they tell you in the presence of your family?

Earl: They told me before the family arrived. But then they took the family aside, and told them, too—the whole facts. And (apologetically) I told you when I talk about it I, I.... (breaks down)

Paul: I know. I know. It gets to you.

   That's the thing that got to me. In fact, you know the first fellow I broke down to is the fellow we're talking to right now on this tape, Larry

Richards. A real good brother of mine. Yeah. He called me the night — I think it was the night before — I was going in for surgery. Anyway, I had done pretty well up to that time. During my chemotherapy I was bad. But I think Larry was the first one I really kinda busted all apart with. And, if you're like I was, there were certain people you wanted to hear from, and certain ones (chuckles) you really didn't. Have you found that?

Earl: Well, no. We don't have that many close friends out here. My wife has never believed much in company, and this has always been a problem. We haven't developed close friends. You know, if you can't have them around or over to your house, you just don't get that close.

Paul: Uh-huh.

Earl: But, right from the start, I really wasn't...wasn't upset. I felt there are two things. One thing, I was sixty years old, and something could have happened to me years ago. My kids are just about grown up, my youngest is fifteen, doing well and all. Good kids.

Another thing is, I had faith in God, and so I didn't really have any reason to....

Paul: You really feel secure in God, don't you, Earl?

Earl: Yeah, I do. I've never been upset myself. Just my family.

Paul: I know it. See, I can relate to that. And I'm not going to have you tell that story that you told me about your son, but boy, that was a heart-rending story. Which tells me what a close family you have.

Earl: He's eighteen.

Paul: Eighteen. And your son was so upset that he said to you, his dad...

Earl: Really, he never told me.

Paul: Oh really?

Earl: I got it round about.

Paul: Oh really?

Earl: Yeah. He was praying to take my place.

Paul: He was praying to take your place? Boy.

Earl: He and I have never talked about it. (Pause)

Paul: Boy, if that isn't something.
    What do you feel, Earl, that helps you when you get down. Does prayer help you? Does that give you strength? Or do you just sort of relax, knowing He's with you? Or do you read anything? Does that. . .

Earl: I read. Different things. The Bible. But I've never really been down very much. I am eager to get preparations made, you know. We have a "quickie" will we drew up, just to cover things in the meantime. Now we're drawing up a more detailed one, where we have a trust set aside for the two boys. More education, and so forth. And I'm eager to get that finished up. But otherwise, I've never really felt down very much.

Paul: You're the type of fellow who's always been even-tempered, and things don't bother you an awful lot. I've noticed that. Boy, if this doesn't bother you, if this doesn't get you down, then nothing in this world will get you down.

Earl: Yeah.

Paul: Do you think it's because of your own nature, or. . . .

Earl: I think it's a combination of my, well, of growing up in a situation where I always fought my own battles all the time. Plus faith in God. 'Cause even people with great faith in God, you know, break down a lot.

Paul: Oh, definitely.

Earl: Ask God what He's doing to them.

Paul: Why do we always blame God, Earl?

Earl: I've never felt that at all.

Paul: No. 'Cause you know, there's an enemy here, according to my Bible, who's caused all the problems. But the end is victory, for us.

Earl: Yeah.

Paul: I think, right now, I've prayed many times for you, for God to give you strength, 'cause you need all the strength that you can...

Earl: Thank you.

Paul: All the strength that you can have, and for your family. Is your wife taking this pretty well?

Earl: Well, she appears to be. My daughter wanted to have lunch with me alone one day. Outwardly, I don't say a great deal.

Paul: Yeah. I know.

Earl: And, she really wanted to know what my faith was.

Paul: I see.

Earl: She wanted to find out.

Paul: Really? That's interesting. You're a silent worshiper, which, to me, many times is the most solid, by a long shot.

Earl: (pause) I think this probably had something to do with my son's feeling, too. He felt that he was better able to handle it, that he had a lot of faith.

Paul: Yeah, I see. Okay, that's why he wanted to take your place. 'Cause he figured that maybe he had more faith than you had. He didn't know that side of you entirely. (Pause) Where did you get this faith?

Earl: Well, it's been shaky, but it's been, well...that was

back some years. An awful long time, I guess. Thirty years or more when I used to go to church, and wonder a lot. Wonder if I was a hypocrite. . . .

Paul: Oh, yeah.

Earl: Yeah. And saying the things I did in church, and so forth. A little rebellious.

Paul: We've all been there.

Earl: But then, I gradually got over that. There was no sudden change, but I've. . .there's enough evidence, you know, miracles that were performed, that. . . .

Paul: (pause) You know, I'm glad to hear that. See, I run across a lot of people who can say, at least they do say, "I was born again at seven o'clock on Tuesday of 1947." You know, I've never had that experience. Mine was like yours, Earl. It just sort of evolved little by little, and I grew, I'm sure by the leading of the Holy Spirit I grew, into a relationship with Jesus Christ that nobody could shake loose from me.

I don't know how people can survive without. . . without a measure of that faith. Anyway. . . . In your own case, you talk about your faith, and your family. Is there any other thing, or person, or factor, which you look to for strength?

Earl: Well, most of my close friends, the friends that are giving me a lot of support, are in Minnesota. I get calls regularly from back there. To see how things are going. (pause) I have one sister, living over near Blue Orchard, and I talk to her quite a lot.

Paul: Now, your daughter you mentioned. Your daughter is a real. . . .

Earl: She's a physician.

Paul: Yeah, I know that. Is she. . .is she a real firm believer?

Earl: I think so. Yeah.

Paul: And that's why she wanted to talk to you? To find out where you were spiritually?

Earl: Yeah.

Paul: See, I didn't know that your whole family.... I knew your wife was spiritually inclined. I knew that you were spiritually inclined. I didn't know about the kids. I'm glad to know that.

I wonder, Earl. I see people who are caught in this situation. And what bothers me is, how can we, we who believe and trust God, pass this on to somebody else?

Earl: Well, it's kind of difficult. You know, unless you're living pretty close to 'em. They don't come to a place where they can learn more about the miracles that Christ performed on earth, and so forth, you know, which no ordinary human could do.

Paul: You believe the Bible.

Earl: Yeah. Uh-huh.

Paul: Now, you're a scientist. How come you believe the Bible? I see a lot of scientists. In fact I was out with one of them the other night, and he said he didn't believe that kind of stuff. Why do you believe?

Earl: I can't go along with some of the explanations. I don't believe the things they come up with, so I don't think it's that difficult.

Paul: But, for example, why do you believe in Jesus?

Earl: (pause) Well, He certainly, as far as I'm concerned, wasn't an ordinary human being.

Paul: By no means.

Earl: I think that's where most belief comes from. And there seems to be enough verification of different parts of the Bible by different people, you know, the same things written independently.

Paul: You wouldn't know who God was if Jesus hadn't

come, would you?

Earl: Yeah. Right.

Paul: You wouldn't know His love. You wouldn't know His power. You wouldn't know His healing capacity.

Earl: It would be difficult to believe this from the Old Testament.

Paul: Oh, yeah. And, above all, you wouldn't know that He was victorious over death, and that you have something to look forward to.

Earl: Right.

Paul: But the bottom line, though, is faith. Isn't it? You know, somebody was saying to me the other night, "Prove it to me." I said, "Hey, man. You're talking to the wrong guy."

Earl: No. It's something you develop.

Paul: That's right. But Earl, here's the thing—I know, I know that this faith that you have is the thing that's going to see you through.

Earl: Yeah. I think so. And that's why it's not more upsetting to me than it is.

Paul: I think that's fantastic. You know mine wasn't as serious a tumor as yours, but for me it was pretty serious. And because it was extensive, they couldn't get it all out surgically, and they told me all those sorts of thing. And so people would come to me and say, "Well, aren't you worried?" And by this time I'd almost forgotten and I'd say, "No, I'm not worried. What is there to worry about?"

Earl: Yeah.

Paul: (chuckling) Either it's there or it isn't there, and there's not a thing worrying's going to do. And I'm not the strongest guy in the world, but I do know this, that I trust God and no matter what happens to me here, I have a bright future. And that's basically what you believe, I'm sure.

Earl: Yeah. You don't get there by works, or anything.

Paul: No, sir. Isn't that the truth. It's strictly a free gift. But see, here you are, Earl. Six months ago you'd never have thought you'd be in this position.

Earl: That's right.

Paul: Came right out of the blue. Which is what happened to me, and can happen to anybody. I don't know whether your faith deepened after that, but I imagine it did.

Earl: I think so. I suppose it did, yeah. Started to think a little more about it.

Paul: Just natural that you did.

Earl: I remember, last evening at home. Eunice had heard a couple of men talking about some psychic help they'd been giving to a lot of cancer patients, to the extent that they'd slowed the growth. And I said, "Well you believe in psychic stuff a lot more than I do." And she said, "Not any more." You know, she used to go to a sort of faith healer, she and her mother. Even though at the same time she'd take medicine, and felt strongly there. But they also thought... well, they're just playing all the angles.
    I really just wasn't interested, and fell asleep.

Paul: I'm perfectly willing to be healed, and so are you, but I'm not demanding it from God.

Earl: No. Nope. I told God from the beginning that He should do what He thinks best.

Paul: What more could we want than that?

Developing Sensitivity

> Personal projects for individuals or study groups to help
> develop sensitivity for ministry with the terminally ill.

1. Reread the experiences shared, taking notes on the needs revealed. In what ways might a caring community provide support and help?

2. In the final dialogue transcript, note the kinds of things that Paul Johnson said which may have helped Earl feel comfortable sharing. What words or phrases might you underline to give you ideas for talking with a life-threatened person?

3. If you would like to obtain audio tapes of interviews between Paul Johnson and others with terminal or life-threatening illnesses, these can be obtained for $4 each from Dynamic Church Ministries, 3596 Bristol Lake Road, Dowling, Michigan 49050. Each C-60 tape contains two interview sessions.

    These tapes can be used for (a) training experiences in study groups, (b) personal listening. In each a patient or former patient talks with Paul about his or her experience with life-threatening illnesses, his needs and how these might be best met, and particularly about the impact of relationship with God in these times of trauma.

    Tapes available are Interview I, and Interview II.

Chapter 6

Communicating Hope

O ne of the most devastating impacts of life-threatening illness is the sudden or gradual theft of hope. Without hope an individual gives up. Though he may not sink into a state of depression, surrender to death will often hasten death. One sensitive book[1] which traces the last months of life of a young woman illustrates the danger: she unquestioningly accepted her doctor's verdict of death, and set about the task of recording her feelings as she died. Whether or not she might have recovered otherwise is, of course, uncertain. But the fact that she had no hope, and was given no reason to hope, would have an impact on her body's response to the disease, and on her personal experience in the illness.

As Paul Johnson points out often, doctors are not God. "I've seen too many persons recover from cancers who should have died, medically speaking, to ever tell anyone they are sure to die."

But hope of recovery is not the only hope that's meaningful to a person who may be terminally ill. There are many ways in which hope plays an important and meaningful role in serious illness.

In this chapter we want to explore something of the nature of the hope which we can offer to those who may be terminally ill, and explore how we can communicate that hope.

But before we can communicate hope, we must have hope ourselves. Dr. David Peters, who shares his own experience with cancer in a Scripps Memorial Hospital Cancer Center film, talks of the way in which others communicate hopelessness. "When you start backing out the door, your eyes are different. When you can't wait to answer that next phone call, they know what you're trying to do."[2] When a person caring for the ill person loses hope, his attitude is communicated in many little ways.

This chapter's exploration of hope, then, is for you as a caring person, as much as it is for a patient. You need to understand the nature of the hope which you can validly hold out, and the nature of the hope you can hold for the person to whom you minister.

Roots of Hopelessness

An insightful chapter in Sharon Roberts's nursing textbook, *Behavioral Concepts and the Critically Ill Patient*, links hopelessness to a loss of control.[3] Individuals who sink into hopelessness feel trapped; they look ahead and see every avenue of choice blocked. Psychiatrists associate this pattern with rigid structures of thought, feeling, and action. No possibilities for personal action or control are envisioned, and without an image of what might be, feelings of futility come to drain the individual of energy and move him toward passive surrender. "The hopeless individual not only feels like 'giving up,' but he actually does," the author says. "He decides that even if he has resources and even if help was available, there is no use, no good, no sense in action or in life. The feeling of hopelessness is a major concern."[4]

Another writer suggests that "hope begins when I have exhausted my own resources and I am drawing on the strength of another."[5] Her point is that when the ill person can no longer hope, those around him must provide a context of hope on which he can draw. This hope need not be the prospect of complete restoration. But it must be hope that the individual can and will reach his full potential within the limits his illness has imposed on him.

Roberts explains that "the key word in helping the critically ill patient overcome his feelings of hopelessness is goal."[6] Paul Johnson stresses this in some of the principles we'll examine shortly, and in simple statements like "I want to get these tests over so we can get you home." The prospect of going home provides a goal toward which the person is moving, and that goal engenders an attitude of hope.

Even for a person who is in the final stages of a terminal illness, this kind of hope can be provided. A friend who promises, "I'll be here tomorrow at two," also introduces a goal, a desired event toward which the individual's life is moving. The prospect of seeing that friend tomorrow is something for which to hope. This, by the way, is why it is so devastating when a person who makes a promise does not come the next day. The visit was a significant goal, a significant symbol of hope. Failure to keep the promise is more than a disappointment; it is a destroyer of the kinds of hope which may yet remain and which are very significant in the life of the ill person.

But there are other aspects to hopelessness. The person sinking into hopelessness sees every avenue of future choice blocked. And typically he has lost decision-making control of his or her present situation as well.

> The critically ill patient relinquishes the ability he normally has of deciding and choosing what he wants or does not want to do. Now someone else, usually a stranger, makes the decisions and choices for him. A dietitian acting on the doctor's order decides the type of food he eats. The hospital decides when he shall eat. His dinner may arrive at 5

P.M., although he usually dines at 7 P.M. The
nurse even decides how the patient shall eat. The patient soon discovers that his daily activities are
tightly scheduled and monitored by other people.
All phases of the day's activities are tightly scheduled, with one activity leading at a prearranged time
into the next, the whole sequence of activities being
imposed from above by a system of explicit formal
rulings and a body of officials.[7]

This description, of course, is of the experience of a
hospitalized patient. But the same problem can exist during
an illness when the person is at home.

Weisman and Hackett have identified a phenomenon they call *premortem dying*, which may occur in
the interactions between the dying person and his
family and may indicate that an anticipatory grieving is taking place. The dying person is less and less
often allowed to participate in decisions regarding
the family or his own interest. Instead, family members frequently respond with "Don't you worry,"
and "Everything is being taken care of" to the dying
person's questions about what is happening outside
the hospital. It is not unusual to observe this phenomenon when dying is prolonged. While family
members generally perceive their behavior as protecting the dying person from participating in stress-
ful situations, such behavior does indicate a change
in the family system and may indicate that they
already think of him as no longer a part of the
family.[8]

This well-meant and gradual divesting of an individual of
decision-making participation and control increases the sense
of helplessness, and the loss of hope. It communicates to the

individual that the family has lost hope for him, and in fact regards him as socially if not physically dead.

We can summarize then, and suggest three primary factors related to hopelessness:

The closing down of the future as a realm of possibility. The future instead seems to be a doorless corridor leading through darkness to one final exit ahead.

A lack of meaningful goals toward which to move. The individual sees himself as helpless to progress toward anything in the future which may have meaning for him, or give him a sense of purpose.

A lack of decision-making control in the present. The individual feels helpless, his daily life and schedule determined by others.

A ministry of caring with those who have life-threatening illnesses involves sensitivity to factors relating to hope. We want to open up the future as a realm of possibility. We believe, and want to help the patient believe, that the corridor into tomorrow *does* have branchings, and may lead to a number of different possible outcomes. We want to provide meaningful goals toward which the individual can move, whatever his medical prognosis. Many of these goals will be short term, and may seem unimportant on the surface. But they must be provided, for they spark the recovery of hope. And finally, we want to protect the right of the individual to exercise as much control as possible over his present, that he might be preserved from that sense of helplessness which also destroys hope.

False Hopes

Cathy is only 36, a young mother and a member of a growing congregation in Spokane, Washington. She has advanced cancer of the liver; a cancer as serious as one can be.

Cathy's gone through chemotherapy and radiation therapy. In the process she lost all her hair, and much strength. She dresses carefully, though, and her wig is shaped to highlight her best features. Makeup hides everything but the strain that shows in her eyes and three tiny vertical wrinkles in the center of her forehead.

She talks openly of her sickness and the difficulty of imagining her children growing up without her. But there are joys, too—joys that show the value of simple hopes. For instance, one couple in the congregation anonymously contributed money so she and her husband could visit Disneyland. They'd always wanted to go. Looking forward to the trip, and savoring it, was important to her. She also tells of all she's learned about prayer. Not so much prayer for herself, but intercessory prayer, as her own anguish has made her sensitive to the suffering of others.

But one thing bothers her. Several people in her congregation have visited to urge her to "claim" healing. "If only you have faith," they tell her, "God will heal you."

One group of three laid hands on her and prayed loudly, claiming to "feel the power" flow into Cathy's body. With the prayer concluded, they announced that Cathy was healed, and insisted that she "claim the healing." "Stand up and praise God that you're healed," Cathy was urged. And all the time Cathy still felt the pain.

To Cathy, who knows that God loves her and is with her, such talk seems far removed from reality. Cathy believes that God *can* make her well. But the attempt of the healers to force her to claim something that she knew was false makes her angry.

"They're really saying that my healing depends on the strength of *my* faith, not on God's goodness or His plan." When Cathy is feeling low, their demands push her toward false guilt. Then Cathy remembers who God is, and what He is like, She knows Him as a loving father, who suffers with her in pain, and who comforts her. She knows God is not some tyrant, demanding impossible feats and withholding a good gift because His child, in the grip of human weakness, cannot achieve what He requires.

It is not wrong to hope in God.

But it is wrong to hold out false hope; a hope that does not honor God with confidence, but seeks to manipulate God by self-energized "faith."

Others, with less faith than Cathy in God's wisdom and love, do seek out healers or places of healing. More often than not these may be secular rather than religious. Cancer patients hear of a clinic in Miami, or Mexico, or a doctor in the Philippines. They put their trust in Laetrile or massive doses of vitamins or in special diets.

Yet it's difficult to deny the terminally ill person even false hope. Dr. David Peters, the physician quoted earlier, who died from cancer in 1979, makes the following observation:

> I, personally, believe that the patient must be given some control over his own life and over his own disease. He got the cancer all by himself. It's his cancer and I think he has some right in saying how that's going to be treated. I remember one time in chemotherapy, I couldn't take any more and the doctor wanted me to take another six months, and I said, "Look, I can't take any more. I'm quitting." He didn't say, well, if you're going to quit I won't take care of you any more. Or, if you quit you're committing suicide. He didn't make me feel guilty. He simply said, "Okay, you're an adult, you can make that decision. Let's find another way." And that gave me some control over my own life. And that brings us to another topic. I really think that Laetrile, wheat grass diets, grape juice diets, bio-feedback, all those things give the patient one thing. They give him control over his own body. He's do-ing something actively for himself—to himself— and if the medical profession gives up hope and

doesn't want to give away that control, the patient's going to find hope somewhere else. And honestly, most patients I know that resort to those unorthodox methods of treatment have gone the route of their own physicians. They've gone through chemotherapy and radiation and surgery, and they've done all that, and you know it and I know it.[9]

The significant point here is seen in Dr. Peters's final comment. "Most patients I know that resort to these unorthodox methods of treatment *have gone the route* with their own physicians." But what if they haven't? The right of the individual to control his own person should be preserved. Yet when a person turns to something which may involve a false hope, and in the process discards a better hope, we have to be concerned. When trust in a new diet leads an individual to throw away his prescription medicine, that individual needs to be confronted, and his physician informed. But still we cannot take away his right to self-determination.

There's a difficult balance here to maintain. Even those hopes which may be rooted in false beliefs can be helpful. And they cannot be denied to an individual, for we can hardly wrest control of the individual's life away from him and force him to a course of action against his will. What we can do is continue to be available, continue to provide support and love. When the visit to the faith healer results in no cure, or trust in the miracle diet fades, we will be more necessary than ever. And hope will continue to be important. But hope, and trust, rooted in reality rather than fantasy.

Hope

Earlier we saw three factors influencing hope and hopelessness: goals, options, and control. To have meaningful goals, to see the future as a realm of possibilities, and to exercise some element of personal control in decisions relating to himself, all counter an individual's hopelessness and encourage hope.

Paul Johnson, as a Christian and a doctor, has found three arenas in which these factors can operate. He seeks to create hope for the present, for the immediate future, and for the eternal future. We can see the interaction in Figure 7 (you may want to fill in the spaces with specifics as you read through the rest of this chapter).

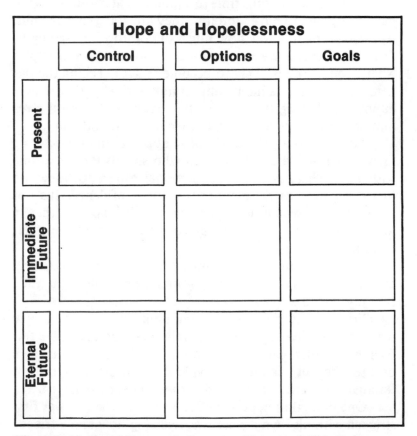

Figure 7. Table of Factors Influencing Hope and Hopelessness.

The Present. The first question is, what kinds of hope for the present can we offer? One is the hope of feeling physically better, through medication, surgery, science, and so forth. This is a very important kind of hope, for pain rapidly drains a person's strength.

It's also important for medical personnel to provide present hope in facing the unknown. Typically a person with a life-threatening illness is acutely sick when in the hospital for tests and initial treatment. The patient is usually confused, and the unknown he is facing today causes intense concern. The doctor needs to take time to explain what sort of tests the patient is going to have, and how they are going to make him feel. He needs to know how much discomfort he is going to feel. Some tests are very exhausting. Unless a person knows what's coming he is likely to become fearful. Telling the patient exactly what is happening to him and why is extremely important. Taking this kind of time with an ill person gives him hope in his doctors, nurses, technicians, and aides.

Many times a patient will have hope not in his doctor or nurse but in his aide, the person who spends the most time with him. There is a strong relational aspect to hope: we fasten on persons as anchors for our confidence. It's not always the one who is doing the most for the ill person that he locks into. It's usually a person with whom he feels comfortable.

This also points up the importance of the love of family and friends. Here too is a vital source of present hope when the future is unknown.

Friends in the Christian community enter here. Today many persons live far from their relatives, and may have few friends. Brothers and sisters from their church, or members of a service club, can help provide the comfort brought by a familiar face and the knowledge that someone really cares.

One thing that impressed Dr. Johnson when he was first stricken with his own cancer was realizing how many friends he had. As he received cards and flowers and telephone calls, he was totally amazed at how many people cared about what happened to him. These little things introduced a special kind of support that is experienced as hope—or at least communicates a great sense of personal significance which battled hopelessness.

It is also important for hope to encourage peace of mind in a person's "today" experience. Recently Dr. Johnson was referred to a patient in the final stages of an advanced cancer of the pancreas. This man's future was measured not in days or weeks but in hours. Dr. Johnson recounts his experience.

"I didn't know this man before, so I had a difficult time in hurriedly understanding where he was. I asked him, 'Are you a believer?' That's a very leading question. I wouldn't do that if I had time with him. But I had to get right to the point, and I felt this was a term he would not recognize or he'd grab on to.

"Well, he grabbed it quick. So I knew that he was a believer. And I said, 'You believe in Jesus?'"

"'Oh yes.'"

"'Mr. Sand, do you realize that you are very seriously ill?'"

"'Yes.'"

"'Do you realize that you have a malignant tumor, which is growing very fast, and that you may not have a lot of time?'"

"'Yes, I realize that.'"

"'I want to talk to you just a moment about your future. I want to do all I can to let you know that I, as a believer too, would like to minister to you in any way that I can and help you. Would you like to see your own minister?'"

"'I don't have a minister.'"

"'Then I'm your minister. I also am your doctor, and I'm going to do everything I can scientifically to help you. But more important than that, I want to affirm your belief, and to reinforce your faith that confidence in Jesus is real. Do you want me to pray with you?'"

"And he said, 'Yeah, I would. I'd like to have you pray with me.'"

"I got right up close, because we were in a ward, and I prayed with him—not very long, but just praying for the

Lord to be with him and give him strength, and to let him know that Jesus was with him and would never leave him.

"I don't know exactly what I said, but the prayer was so he could have real peace, right there. I don't know any other way, when medicine is failing as it was failing him then, but to get right to the point, real quick."

Immediate future. One of the most significant ways to encourage hope is to recognize the desire of most people to return to familiar surroundings. Dr. Johnson focuses attention on getting the patient out of the hospital and back home. This is one thing you can talk about, and Johnson says, "I see patients who really light up when I say, 'You know, I think you're going to get to go home in about three or four days!'"

Patients will often not ask because they don't want to be disappointed. So medical personnel need to take the initiative, even if the disease is incurable. Normally the patient can be taken care of at home as well as at the hospital.

What is it about returning home that is important to most people? There you can eat the foods you enjoy, prepared the way you like them; you can be in your normal surroundings; you can even engage in your normal activities. For many the prospect of getting back to their place of work is very significant. Even if they are unable to work they want to know what's going on there.

All these are to be stressed as possibilities. They may not all come to pass, but they are possibilities. The future is *not* closed.

Even if the individual cannot affect the ultimate outcome of the disease, he can and should have some control over what is going to happen to him all during the time he has left.

The promise of control is very important to extend... and to keep. Paul Johnson has an older patient who has previously undergone surgery, and has now returned with cancer well-established in her lymphatic system. In a case like hers, the immediate future should normally involve chemotherapy or radiation or both. But she doesn't want that. She had such treatment earlier, and became very sick from the radiation. She said, "I don't want to go through that, and I don't want to go through chemotherapy." She thought Paul Johnson was going to give her a battle. But he said, "You know what, you don't have to go through that. You know as well as I that your chances are probably a little bit better with medication. However, that's no guarantee either. If you don't want those things, you don't have to have those things. You know as well as I that your prognosis is guarded. But we don't know very much about your immediate future. And I can tell you one thing! This is not going to be life-threatening for a while, even if you don't do anything."

So her immediate future holds a plus. And here too we can stress the positive possibilities. Paul Johnson notes, "We *don't* know. If we do nothing for this woman, she might live as long or even longer than if we would treat her, because this is a disease we freely admit we don't have the answers for."

The hope that is important to this woman is the hope that she will live *comfortably*. She wants to function, and her past experience with radiation has led her to choose what is important to her.

Many who have incurable diseases hope that science will advance soon enough to take care of them. In many instances, they're right! So this is a hope based on some rather sound thinking. If they have a disease which is slow in developing, it's very possible an effective medical treatment will turn up. Diseases which were incurable not many years ago can be treated today with great success.

The family is also important for the immediate future, if there's a good family relationship. Most of the time there is someone in the family the person relates to, and receives support from. At times it may be someone who acts like family, such as a very close friend.

By and large the person who is looking to the immediate future is hopeful of returning to a productive life. Being able to contribute in the family, being able to make his own bed and care for his own needs, are goals with great meaning to the seriously ill. For some in the hospital, even to shave or feed themselves is a significant achievement and a positive step toward depression-relieving hope.

Before we look at hope in relation to eternity, there are several more principles to stress in thinking about hope for the immediate present. In *The Psychiatrist and the Dying Patient*, Eissler notes the importance of time and of an individual's *psychological present*. This is the *span of time* which is experienced as "present" by him, and will vary between different persons. For some, who focus on long term projects, the present may be five or even ten years. For others the present is three or six months. For a child the present may be the next half hour. The helping person, Eissler suggests, needs to discover what span of time represents the "present" to an ill person, and help him to live within that time frame.

One organization we'll look at in another chapter, Make Today Count, concentrates on helping persons under serious stress focus on *today* as the present, to find meaning within that time frame.

This approach is valid and wise. None of us control our future, nor live in it. Nor can we live in the past. "The present time is of the highest importance" (Romans 13:11, Phillips) is a helpful biblical reminder. God gives us the present in which to live, and it is in our present that life is to have meaning and purpose.

It is also in the present that we can know the comfort of God's love. "Surely I will be with you always" is the Scripture's great reminder that, as we move through time, we never reach a present in which we are isolated from God's love. As we seek to develop ministering relationships with those who have serious illnesses, we need to believe with them that their present *is* meaningful, whatever the future may hold. Holding this belief and confidence, we can with honesty be optimistic for them in our offer of hope.

Eternal future. The Christian is convinced that each human being has an eternal destiny. Human life is too significant to God, and individuals made in His image are too highly valued, to fade away to nothingness. Human personality and self-consciousness continue beyond the death of the body, and are destined once again to be united with a body in the resurrection foretold by God in the Scriptures. The promise of God's presence in our present, in the immediate future, and forever, is a reality that gives both life and death unique meaning. Thus in our relationship with the terminally ill, members of the caring Christian community hold out hope for life beyond physical death.

At this point *staying with* a person is particularly significant. It's common, when a serious illness strikes an individual, for many friends and acquaintances to rally around. But as the months pass and sometimes extend into years, typically only the family continues concerned. Continuing to be available and to care, over time, is a vital aspect in communicating God's own stability and continuing love. And communicating God's love in practical, personal ways is vital to sharing the gospel's message in words.

How do we sensitively communicate the good news to others? All too often Christians use an overeager approach which may almost frighten others. In general a gradual, even humble approach is most helpful. Paul Johnson's experience with a Washington state senator illustrates his own approach to sharing Christ and the gospel's hope for eternity.

The senator, whom we will call Senator Powell, was very well known in the community. He was very proud of his position, and wanted everyone to address him as "Senator." If you didn't he would correct you immediately.

He was also the editor of a successful neighborhood newspaper, and chairman of the hospital board.

"So here was a man who died when he was about sixty, and everyone was afraid of him because his way was domineering, ugly, almost mean. When he was chairman of a committee, it went his way. He was a very unpleasant man to be around.

"I had worked with him on several committees, and so knew him. He developed a neck cancer that spread rather rapidly. He was hospitalized, and having known him and that he was in real dire straits, I went in to talk to him.

"I said, 'Senator Powell, I just want to come in and tell you I'm really sorry you're sick.' When I told him, I felt it was probably the last chance I'd have to make any impression on him so far as his future was concerned. I felt fairly certain he was not very familiar with any spiritual things. So I said, 'Senator, you're in real trouble, and you know that. I just want to share with you what I believe. It may not make any sense to you, but I want to share what I believe, and if it would give you any support, that would really make me feel good.

"'You know, I happen to believe that Jesus Christ is the Son of God. He was here, He revealed God's love to us. And not only that, He recognized we're all sinners, and He came to provide a way we can be reconciled to God.

"'For that, He had to die on the cross, and He did die, for you and for me. Our behavior isn't going to be the key to whether we live again. . . it's how we relate to Jesus Christ, the Son of God.'

"I went through that with him, and he didn't say anything. His face was very stern; he showed no reaction at all, but just looked straight ahead. So I said, 'I hope you start feeling better, but I just wanted to share that with you.' And I left. I had no way of knowing how he had reacted; in fact, I thought he had probably resented it.

"The next morning I came into the hospital very early. When I came in I was being paged. I called the operator, and she said, 'Senator Powell wants you in his room.'

"I thought maybe I was going to go in there and he was going to tear me apart. But when I went in, he said, 'Dr. Johnson, nobody has ever talked to me like that before.'"

"I said, 'Really? Well, what did you think of it?'"

"'Anybody who has ever talked to me in any religious way has been a man of the cloth, and all he wants is money. He's never been interested in my "soul," or where I'm going, or anything like that. How come you're interested in me?'"

"I said, 'Because you're a friend of mine. And what's more, I just want to be sure you know the Good News of the Gospel, because it is good news. It provides something nobody else can provide. Science apparently is not doing so good for you. Man isn't really coming through, and he's not solving your problem. So you have to look somewhere else, and the only place I know you can look that has any value at all is in what God has provided. And that's through Jesus Christ His Son, who really cares for you, whether you know it or not.'"

"That totally disarmed him, and he said, 'You know, I'd like to know more about that.' I said, 'You know, you're opening up to something that's been kept from you for all these years. And I just want to pray with you. Do you mind if I pray with you?'"

"He said, 'No!'"

"I think that was probably the first prayer he'd ever heard in his behalf.

"I saw him daily after that, and when he left the hospital he said, 'I want you to come visit me.'"

"I told him, 'I will. In fact, I'll visit you every day.' So I went and visited him, and we talked about eternal things. There was a TV program that laid out the Gospel that he watched when I wasn't there. He watched, and then he'd have questions. Impossible questions. About the universe, and the cosmos. And all I could say was, 'You're asking questions I can't answer. But you know who made all this? The one who's interested in you.'

"I'd say, 'The thing I do know, He's the only one who came out of the grave.'"

"He'd say, 'You really believe that?'"

"I'd say, 'I know that. I don't just believe, I know that.'"

"He'd say, 'How do you know that?'"

"I'd say, 'It boils down really to faith. I wasn't there. But you know, I wasn't there when George Washington was president either, but I know he was president.'"

"He was a good reporter, so that kind of held together for him.

"He died shortly after that, and I really believe he came to faith. I feel sure I'm going to see Senator Powell in the Kingdom, and I'm going to have a neat time talking with him. And he's going to be so glad that I came into his room."

In this experience Paul Johnson was more direct than normal, but he still followed several important practices. Normally Paul's approach involves much listening to find out where people are, to sense how open and receptive they may be. In Paul's experience, "many people are not receptive to the Gospel at all, initially. They will often even be antagonistic. Some are angry at God about their condition. Others don't believe in God, and are even antagonized by the fact you believe in God. They don't understand God's nature at all, or know who He is. Many—a majority—have just existed and never given Him a thought. Or have been given the wrong introduction to God through the churches. So often much misinformation needs to be *undone,* and you are in fact trying to communicate this eternal hope from below zero. So you must be very careful."

The practices Paul Johnson has found helpful are:

(1) Listen. Listening not only shows respect, it earns a hearing. Often listening will provide clues to the best way to share.

(2) Don't impose. Paul's way of saying "this makes sense to me; it may not to you," is a powerful weapon. First, it assures the individual that his right to accept or reject the gospel message is fully respected. There will be no attempt to frighten, coerce, or force agreement. Second, it casts the sharing in the form of personal witness. There is no arguing over doctrine here; instead there is simply the affirmation of personal faith. For either medical personnel or a person who

has proven himself to care, and thus earned respect, such a witness carries significant weight.

(3) Stress personal benefits. Paul Johnson tends to focus on the individual's present experience. Faith in Christ brings significant comfort. Man's effects, and science's advances, are finally reaching their limits. There's a reason then to explore the possibility that a God who is greater than men and science exists and loves you.

(4) Focus on personal relationship. It's important in sharing the Gospel to keep the focus on the Person of Jesus and His love for each individual. Church affiliation and denominational distinctives all fade to insignificance in view of the individual's need for a personal relationship with God through Jesus Christ. That Jesus is the Son of God, died for the individual, and loves him now, is the heart of the good news we share.

In each dimension of the ill individual's life—his present, his immediate future, and his eternal future—there *is* hope. Those in the caring community approach ministry to the life-threatened with this confidence, and so enter a relationship with the ill with positive expectations. We also know there are keys to communicating hope; keys which operate whatever our relationship with the individual. In our relationship we do respect the individual's right of self-determination, and resist the tendency to wrest control from him or her. In our relationship we focus on options the future holds as positive possibilities for the individual. And in our relationships we help the individual set goals toward which he or she can move.

In our ministering relationship we can use these keys to bring hope into the present experience, the immediate future, and the eternal destiny of the seriously ill.

Developing Sensitivity

> Personal projects for individuals or study groups to help develop sensitivity for ministry with the terminally ill.

1.   Jot down (without rereading) as many causes of the loss of hope as you can remember. Beside each, jot down some tools or approaches a person might use to help restore hope. Finally review the chapter, checking your answers, and fill in the chart on page 111 as completely as possible.

2.   The ultimate basis for the hope we can offer any individual is provided by sharing Jesus Christ and his love. Reread Paul's experience with the state senator, and observe how the witnessing principles he's found significant were applied (pp. 117-21). What in the experience seems most helpful to you?

Chapter 6, Notes

1. JoAnn K. Smith, *Free Fall* (Valley Forge, Pa.: Judson Press, 1975).

2. Dr. David Peters, "From Both Ends of the Telescope," *San Diego Physician* (October 1979): 33.

3. Sharon L. Roberts, *Behavioral Concepts and the Critically Ill Patient* (Englewood Cliffs, N.J.: Prentice-Hall, Inc., 1976), p. 116f.

4. Ibid., p. 163.

5. Sister Madeleine Clemence Vaillat, "Hope: The Restoration of Being," *American Journal of Nursing*, 70 (February 1970): 272.

6. Roberts, *Behavioral Concepts*, p. 175.

7. Ibid., p. 123.

8. Carol Ren Kneisl, "Grieving: A Response to Loss," in *The Dying Patient: A Supportive Approach*, ed. Rita E. Caughill (Boston: Little, Brown and Co., 1976) p. 38.

9. Peters, "Both Ends," p. 34.

Chapter 7

Being a Friend

I remember well the day I heard that Paul Khale's brother, a Missionary Aviation Fellowship pilot, had been killed in West Irian. I went over to Paul and Mary's house, feeling more uncertain about how I should react than feeling for them. It was a painful experience; I talked woodenly, said the right things and quickly left. Later I heard they had asked each other, "Why did he come?" My own discomfort in the situation was so great that I hadn't been able to comfort them.

It's no surprise that we are often uncertain in our relationships with the life-threatened. Whether we are family or neighbor or a member of a helping profession (such as doctor, nurse, or social worker), our own painful uncertainty can block our ability to help and support. So it's helpful to gain some perspective on how to relate one-to-one, and to simply be a friend.

The testimony of many helps us realize that friendship is important. In spite of our uncertainties, there is an important role for simple friendship. One young student nurse, dying of a malignancy, sensed the fears of those around her and wrote this appeal.

I know you feel insecure, don't know what to say, don't know what to do. But please believe me, if you care, you can't go wrong. Just admit that you care. That is really for what we search. We may ask for why's and wherefore's, but we don't really expect answers. Don't run away—wait—all I want to know is that there will be someone to hold my hand when I need it.[1]

Randy Becton tells of the friendship of a co-worker, Landon Saunders, and what that friendship meant in his own struggle with cancer.

Landon accepted me just as I was through this experience. When I was lonely, or frightened, or doubting, or faithless, or brave, or callous, he always affirmed my personal worth. God's servant will accept people where they are and love them for what they are. He loved whether I was lovable or not. He sought to understand this experience from my perspective, to identify with my feelings. Yet, more than simply empathizing, he sought to bring the loving correction of God's truth, His will, into my heart at every opportunity. God's servant helps people face reality, helps them see God's way to face life and death. He sought to stand on the rock foundation of trust in Jesus Christ and to help me stand on it, when it appeared that all around was sinking sand.

His liability for me was total. He didn't worry about protecting his emotions, keeping emotional involvement at arm's length. He got involved, totally, and risked the possibility of getting hurt. He was completely willing to experience with me the "valley of the shadow of death."[2]

In each case the need was simply for someone to care, someone to be a friend. And, despite our very natural hesitation, being a friend isn't a difficult task.

Communication

Communicating love and concern is at the heart of the friendship that the life-threatened need. There are a number of simple yet important guidelines we can follow that lead to significant communication.

Full attention. When I visited Paul Khale and his wife after their tragedy, I wasn't ready to give them my full attention. Instead I was focused on my own discomfort. They very quickly picked up that my concern about how I should react kept me from focusing on them!

There are a number of ways to let a person know we're giving him or her our full attention. We sit down in the room rather than remain standing. We draw up our chair closer rather than keep space between us. We maintain good eye contact, and smile or nod in response to his words. Each of these very simple things says loudly that the other person is important; that we are concentrating our attention on him rather than on ourselves.

Being a friend doesn't require hours of visiting or sitting with an individual, although there may be some times when this is helpful. Usually a consistent regular visit—daily or weekly depending on the situation—is more desirable. Giving full attention for ten or fifteen minutes is, as one writer says, "a key that unlocks the door of his loneliness."[3]

Listening. It's often difficult for friends or relatives to listen sensitively. Their own needs may so dominate that they can't really pay attention to the needs of the patient. Kübler-Ross tells of one situation in which the husband had been completely unable to accept his wife's terminal illness. He had struggled to hold her, pleading that he and the children needed her at home again.

> When I asked him about the patient's needs, rather than his own, he sat in silence. He slowly began to realize that he never listened to her needs but took it for granted that they were the same.[4]

Sensitive listening seeks to discern what the person wants to talk about, and what he or she needs to share. This will vary with individuals and with situations. At times a person will want only small talk, or to share dreams of what life will be like "when I get better." At other times emotions like those Randy Becton described—loneliness, fright, doubt, bravery, callousness, faithlessness—will emerge. Then the individual may want to talk about his or her fears, and the emotions he is experiencing right then.

It's not good to probe for such feelings. Normally a person with a life-threatening illness will desire to share on a deeper level with a few people, but will not want to share deeply with all who call. Genuine interest and compassion, a willingness to talk about whatever the person wants to discuss, and a companionship of "being there" without many words, are ministries as important as that of deeply entering into the experience.

Listening sensitively means focusing on the thoughts and feelings expressed by the individual, and being willing to respond to them. If a person mentions his doubts or fears, it's often good to respond with a statement or question that shows we're willing to talk with him about them. "That must be disappointing for you," or "Do you feel depressed often?" are simple responses that open the door to whatever the individual may want to share.

On the other hand, if the person turns away at the mention of doubts or fears, or quickly changes the subject, you can once again follow his or her lead. Your willingness to talk about the darker aspects of the experience will have been demonstrated. When the individual is ready, that door will open to you again.

Understanding something of the "stages" discussed in chapter 3 is helpful. We'll be able to recognize symptoms of denial, anger, bargaining, depression, and acceptance. Understanding each type of response as normal will help us not to pull back or hide when an individual expresses feelings. And it will help us realize that we should never force another person to talk about his illness unwillingly.

But sensitive listening involves more than discerning how an individual feels. It also involves responding in an accepting or supportive way. There is sometimes a difficult balance to maintain. We want to share our own feelings...but we want most of all to let the other person know that his feelings have been heard and are accepted. Usually we can reflect back the feelings expressed in some simple way, and thus let the person know he's been heard. Here are some common statements that a person with a life-threatening illness might make, and possible responses that reflect acceptance. Notice in the longer patterns that typically a person who is reflecting incorrectly will be corrected by the speaker.

"I get so tired of just lying here."
"You're feeling depressed a lot."

• • •

"The doctors say I'll be out of here next week, but what do they know?"
"You hope they're right, but you're afraid they might not be telling you the truth?"

• • •

"It isn't fair! My kids need me. This shouldn't be happening to me."
"You're worried about your children."

"No, not really. I know Jim will take good care of them. But I shouldn't have to miss all those growing up years."

"It makes you sad to think of them possibly growing up without you there."

"Sometimes I catch myself crying. But usually I feel, well, I just get all burned up about it."

"You mean you get mad. It makes you angry to think of the kids growing up and maybe you not being there."

"Yes, it does. I've been a good Christian, and always tried to do what's right. So why me? God just isn't being fair and, well, I do get angry about it."

"You get angry at God sometimes."

"Yes, I do. Do you think that's terrible?"

In these illustrations we see something of the nature of reflection, and why it's helpful. Reflection puts what the other person is trying to express in different words, and lets the person know that he or she is being heard, not just listened to. Reflective listening does one more thing. As in the longer dialogue above, it keeps the door open to further sharing. It helps the individual express his feelings and put his experience into words, when other kinds of reactions might not do so.

Sometimes sensitive listening is all that's required from a friend. But often you'll want to go beyond showing that you have heard, to reveal something of your reaction. Here it's important for us to realize again that we are called into *nonjudgmental* relationships with the terminally ill. We are not called to react with shock, to condemn, or to let the other person feel that he or she has failed to handle his difficulty in a "Christian" way. Instead, we are to realize that as Christians, we should love others where they are. In each situation we can share, without condemnation, in a supportive way.

How, for instance, might we go beyond reflection in each of the three brief cases quoted above? How might we open up something of our own lives, and communicate caring and hope? Let's trace out these conversations just a bit further.

"I get so tired of just lying here."

"You're feeling depressed a lot."

"Why not? It's hopeless, isn't it?"

"I think if I were in your situation, I'd have times when I felt depressed and hopeless, too. Even though I know God still loves me and hasn't abandoned me."

"Yes, I try to remember that. But sometimes God just feels so far away."

(Reaching out and taking hold of hand.) "Would you like it if we prayed together, right now?"

(Turning head away) *"Not now. But would you ... well, would you pray for me about 10 P.M. each night? That's when it seems to be hardest for me."*

• • •

"The doctors say I'll be out of here next week, but what do they know?"

"You hope they're right, but afraid they might not be telling you the truth?"

"How do I know if they're telling me everything? I hear them talking out there in the hall, and ... well, I imagine all sorts of things."

"Is there any way I can help?"

"No. Well, maybe. Could you talk to the doctor, or someone, and find out? You'd tell me the truth, wouldn't you?"

"Yes. I'll see if I can find out anything and I will tell you the truth. You know, even if it's as bad as you fear, I know the Lord will help you so I'm not afraid of the truth."

• • •

"It isn't fair! My kids need me. This shouldn't be happening to me."

"You're worried about your children."

"No, not really. I know Jim will take good care of them. But I shouldn't have to miss all those growing up years."

"It makes you sad to think of them possibly growing up without you there."

"Sometimes I catch myself crying. But usually I feel, well, I just get all burned up about it."

"You mean you get mad. It makes you angry to think of the kids growing up and maybe you not being there."

"Yes, it does. I've been a good Christian, and always tried to do what's right. So why me? God just isn't being fair and, well, I do get angry about it."

"You get angry at God sometimes."

"Yes, I do. Do you think that's terrible?"

"Well, maybe if I'd never read the psalms I might think it was terrible. But, you know, David and other godly people had times when they were angry at God. God understands that, so why should I think it's terrible?"

"Well, I have a hard time with that myself. I get angry, and then I feel guilty and ashamed."

"You think you shouldn't be angry."

"Don't you?"

"I think God knows how weak we human beings are, and that God isn't upset with us when we're flooded with feelings we can't control. But I also think you'll get past that anger."

"You think so?"

"I really do."

Listening, then, involves paying full attention to the person we're with, and being sensitive to the feelings he expresses. Sensitive listening goes beyond this, and lets him know that we hear his feelings and accept them. We can do this by reflecting his feelings, and by going beyond to show our understanding.

Touching. While listening is one of the most important ways that we can show others we care, it's not the only way. One of the most important is touching. Stroking a person's arm, or holding his hand, can communicate on a very deep level. Every one of us has times when silent companionship, and not conversation, is what is desired.

Praying. We've mentioned prayer briefly on a number of occasions. Now we need to say specifically that brief, warm prayers affirming God's love and asking that the ill person sense His presence, are important avenues of communication and ministry. Kübler-Ross, who has trained many in the helping professions to minister to the terminally ill, comments, "I have seen few who avoided the issue or who showed as much hostility or displaced anger as I have seen among other members of helping professions. What amazed me, however, was the number of clergy who felt quite comfortable using a prayer book or chapter from the Bible as the sole communication between them and the patients, thus avoiding listening to their needs and being exposed to questions they might be unable or unwilling to answer."[5]

But in the context of real listening and a growing sensitivity to where the individual is, prayer is a most meaningful way to communicate love.

One chaplain, Daniel C. DeArment, suggests that prayer is "a way of allowing the patient to experience a feeling of intimacy, while minimizing the risk of further isolation and fear of ego-loss."[6] He is saying that at times talking, and sharing feelings that a person is ashamed of, is threatening. Yet resisting sharing cuts off the possibility of intimacy, because the patient is not able to operate in an open awareness setting (see pages 16 and following). Without open awareness neither person is able to freely share his or her true self. But the patient still has a very deep need for intimacy; for belonging, and for a sense of closeness. In prayer two people can draw close to each other and to God. In a quiet moment of prayer the barriers can be let down and the sense of God's presence experienced together.

Are there any general guidelines for prayer when visiting the terminally ill? First, prayer is a person-to-person ministry that each of us can offer. It doesn't belong simply to the "professional." Each believer *is* a minister, and prayer is one of the simplest and yet most significant ways in which we can serve. Second, our prayers should express positive hopes for the individual. As we saw in the last chapter, there are many dimensions of hope. If we have taken the time to listen sensitively, we should be able to sense the point at which the patient is in greatest need of hope. We can thus focus our prayers on that area of concern. Third, the ministry of prayer involves coming with another person to God, to focus on who He is as well as to share our requests. Prayer with the life-threatened should affirm the goodness, the love, and the other attributes of God which give the believer confidence in Him.

Prayer times need not be long: just a few brief moments bending close, holding hands, and affirming God's love and care for the individual. This is one of our most important ways to be a friend.

Special Problems

Being a friend is essentially a very natural thing. Listening, touching, giving our full attention, praying — all these are simple things that any of us can offer to another. It takes no special training or official "helping profession" role to be a friend to a person with a life-threatening illness. And each of the skills we have explored is something that can be applied in any relationship, whether between doctor and patient, family members, minister and parishioner, or simply friend to friend. Yet it would be unfair to move into such a friend relationship without awareness of two particular problems which the person seeking to minister may face. The problems can be overcome. But they should be understood.

Dealing with personal feelings. In an earlier quote, Kübler-Ross commented on personal feelings she has observed in those who have relationships with the terminally ill. These she described as "hostility or displaced anger." In the first chapters of this book we saw that many times those who work with the life-threatened wall them off, or treat them as children, or in other ways show that the helper himself is so uncomfortable with death and dying he must deal with his own needs rather than be sensitive to the needs of the ill person.

Sometimes personal fears associated with death and dying dominate in an individual's relationship with the life-threatened. This can mean merely discomfort and uncertainty about how to relate, because death is strange to us. When this is all that's involved, usually some understanding of how to approach the relationship will help an individual work through the discomfort stage. Maintaining awareness of the many aspects of hope that we can validly hold for the life-threatened, with sensitive listening, can help such an individual grow more comfortable in the helping and friendship role.

But at times personal fears go beyond uncertainty and general discomfort. Contact with the life-threatened may be a frightening reminder of personal mortality. In such cases a variety of reactions are possible. There is likely to be the masked hostility and anger that Kübler-Ross describes. In doctors and nurses, this may stem from an orientation to health care that demands healing as the only acceptable out-come. The person who is dying in spite of all that medical science can do may be resented or even hated as a symbol of personal failure. Or he may be resented as "taking up time" which might be better spent on someone "who can be really helped."

For family members the threat of separation from the loved one may be so great that their own fears of death dominate. They find it difficult to be sensitive, to listen, to respond to the patient's needs because they are struggling with their own needs. It's a well-documented phenomenon that typically a person with a life-threatening illness faces the realities of his situation more quickly than the family. When the individual is ready to put aside denial, for example, fam-ily members seldom are. The individual may have worked through anger — if he or she experienced that "stage" — while family members are gripped by it. At times the personal needs and fears of the family members make it difficult for them to listen sensitively and offer hope. This fact makes ministry to the family a vital part of ministry to the terminally ill person himself.

Still others in contact with the life-threatened struggle with death and dying on a much more intimate level. Whether friends or members of helping professions, they seek relation-ships with the terminally ill because of *their own* needs rather than the needs of the ill person. More than one person has volunteered to help, or chosen a helping career, because he or she is deeply afraid of death and hopes that somehow such relationships will help him deal with his own terrors.

It's important, then, that a person who will be in a help-ing relationship as a professional or as a friend explore his own attitudes toward death and dying. Here Christian faith makes a vital contribution. While death brings its sorrows, we do not sorrow in the same way as others who have no hope (I Thessalonians 4:13). Instead the Christian approaches death with a perspective transformed by trust in God, and with an outlook shaped by Scripture. For the Christian hope is rooted in God's promise of everlasting love. God's love never lets us go, even in the most difficult circumstances. God's love affirms each human being, and so says that no one is without personal worth and value. For the Christian who understands his faith, the threat of death or disability cannot rob him of hope or of a sense of worth. Resting in the love of God, who has promised to be with us always, the believer can face tomorrow without fear of abandonment.

In addition, death is not viewed by the believer as life's end. Each person has a personal identity that will exist for-ever, as man's destiny stretches beyond this life into eternity. Each human being is too valuable, as an individual made in the image of God, to fade to nothingness. God, the Creator and Sustainer of the universe and the Redeemer of His creatures, has promised resurrection and a world to come. With this confidence we can face the prospect of death. We recognize it as an enemy, but as an enemy whose ultimate defeat is assured.

In chapter 9, which outlines ways to help train indi-viduals for a helping relationship, you'll notice that the first processes are designed to help those being trained to examine their own personal attitudes toward death. Until we each have come to grips with the meaning that death has for us as an individual, it is likely to be very difficult to deal personally with those suffering from a life-threatening illness.

Responding to anger and attack. Much of the literature on death and dying deals with the impact of the reaction of anger to terminal illness. Rather than feeling anxiety, the

individual feels and/or expresses hostility.[7] Hostility is likely
to be expressed toward any handy object or person. Even
when an individual actively seeks to help, he or she may be
rewarded with cutting and unkind words or outbursts of
anger.

It's all too natural and too easy to react with a corre-
sponding hostility, or to become hurt and withdraw. In fact it
takes considerable grace to continue being supportive when a
person we are ministering to not only fails to appreciate what
we're doing but even attacks us.

It helps greatly if we understand the roots of the hostility, and see attacks as revealing deep need. Roberts sums up
factors that research has shown lead to the development of
hostility as follows:

> First, a person experiences frustration, loss of self-
> esteem, or unmet needs for status and prestige. The
> patient experiences frustration in the restriction of
> illness. His self-esteem becomes threatened as he is
> thrust into a forced dependency role. If he was a
> socially prestigious individual who enjoyed self-
> achieved status, he has difficulty accepting depend-
> ent relationships with his doctor and nurse. He may
> continually inform his nurse of his social signif-
> icance and become hostile when she does not re-
> spond with awe. To the critical care nurse, the pa-
> tient is no more or less significant than all other pa-
> tients on the unit. The patient may try to over-
> compensate for his dependency by frequently in-
> forming all concerned who and what he is. His
> behavior is simply a way to reassure himself and
> strengthen his bruised or threatened self-concept.
>
> Second, hostility develops where a situation oc-
> curs in which the patient has certain expectations of
> himself or others. A critically ill patient may place
> tremendous hope in those providing his care.
> Because of irreversible pathology, they may be
> unable to restore him to a previous level of wellness.

Consequently he will be disappointed that his expectations are unmet. He may also hold certain expectations of himself that cannot be fulfilled.

In the third place, the patient may feel inadequate, hurt, or humiliated. As a result, he experiences hostility. Finally, he can experience anxiety, which takes the form of anger. Kiening identifies three different ways in which a patient can respond on an action level: (1) repression and withdrawal; (2) disowning the feeling and overreacting by being extremely polite and compliant; or (3) engaging in some type of overtly hostile behavior, either verbal or nonverbal.[8]

How helpful to realize when a person strikes out at us in anger that the cause of his action is likely to be fear, disappointment, and hurt.

All too often those who deal with the life-threatened are not able to look beyond the anger to the patient's needs. Family members, friends and medical personnel alike are hurt by attacks. They may begin to avoid the patient, to rationalize, or to focus on their own feelings and react rather than minister to the patient.

How do we respond to a hostile person? First, realize that he most likely is acting out of his own personal needs. Very possibly if we were in his situation, we might feel hostility as well. Second, we should listen carefully and sensitively. It's possible that the anger is focused on something that can be corrected: a change in diet, more flexibility in sleep schedule, etc. Hostile reactions are not necessarily "psychological"...they may be rooted in a behavior of others which can and should be changed. It may be that others near the patient are treating him or her as socially dead, and that hostility is the only way the person has found to obtain a reaction from them. So careful listening, seeking the cause of the hostility, can be important.

In our relationship with the patient, our goal as a friend and ministering person is to help him or her work through his feelings to a more effective way of dealing with reality. To do this, we need to be willing to continue to care even when hostility is directed toward us, and to seek ways that we can show the individual we care for him and accept him anyway.

Relational Principles

Against the general background of friendship that we've outlined in this chapter, Paul Johnson suggests a number of principles that he's found to be important over the years. Some of these principles relate directly to medical personnel; others relate to family and friends. Here are Paul's suggestions.

Medical care personnel. The following will help develop and maintain a supportive personal relationship between doctors and nurses and those with a life-threatening illness.

(1) Bring the patient into the decision-making process. It's wrong to simply tell a person "this is what we've got to do." A relationship of mutual respect means informing the patient of choices that need to be made, and helping him or her see the options that exist. A doctor can guide an individual in this process to the medically desirable choice. But this must come as part of a process, and convincing must come through informing. This is the only way to keep the patient from feeling subject to the doctor, and thus threatened by him significantly.

(2) Never discuss reports or medical information in scientific terms. Patients with life-threatening illnesses will be apprehensive. If things of a technical nature must be discussed, it's better to do this outside his room, or to explain carefully what is being talked about.

(3) Make the physical surroundings compatible with the state of the disease. For instance, avoid having a seriously ill person in a room where another, who is not as sick, is watching a loud TV.

(4) Never communicate an attitude of hopelessness. This attitude is often communicated non-verbally. The patient

begins to suspect that the doctor or nurse has little time for him because he is past hope. Or the medical people begin to avoid his room. Often in our hospitals today medical personnel *do* give up on patients, and their behavior then communicates this fact. No matter how serious a person's disease, ministering to him as a whole person means that giving full attention and listening sensitively is a part of the physician's ministry. Even if death itself is certain, there *are* other kinds of hope that can honestly be held out.

(5) Grant any request within reason. Often little things — like a favorite food — mean much to an ill person. It's foolish to insist on TV off or no sugars when the individual's life is threatened, and the extra hours of sleep or the sweets will make no real difference in the course of his disease. Increasingly, hospitals recognize this fact. Little things are important to the individual, and respecting his or her wishes is significant to the total relationship with the patient.

(6) Avoid depersonalizing. Medical people find it easy to think of and speak about patients in an impersonal way. Rather than using names (Mr. Brown), a nurse or doctor may refer to "Bed 367" or "the patient in room 17." The over-familiar use of first names is also to be avoided. When a patient is very sick, and near helplessness, some medical personnel not only treat the individual as a young child but begin to speak to and think of him as a child. Being a friend to those in need means continuing the symbols of respect that an individual in serious condition often needs for ego-support.

Some individuals may want a first name relationship with doctors and nurses and aids. Others will find it most helpful to their own sense of significance if medical personnel use last names.

(7) Do not invade privacy. Freedom for the person to be by himself or herself, and to have the sense of privacy in the hospital setting, is important. A knock on the door before entering is a simple thing, yet can mean much to the patient.

Each of these seven suggestions for medical personnel is designed to give respect to the patient as a person, and to maintain that respect as a basis for the relationship. Friendship implies a relationship of equals: equal in value and importance as persons. When medical personnel rob a patient of significance by treating him without the respect implicit in the suggestions above, an unhealthy relationship will develop, and the ministry of caring that might be offered will be distorted and possibly destroyed.

Family, friends and others. Medical personnel need to remember to treat patients as persons, not as objects. Those who already know a person with a life-threatening illness will have established some level of friendship with them. Yet they too need to be careful that, under the strain of the life-threatening illness, the bonds of friendship and love do not become distorted. Paul Johnson shares these suggestions which also grow out of his thirty years as physician and friend to thousands of people with terminal illnesses.

(1) Don't let love depersonalize. Sometimes we love others too much. This may be expressed by trying to take on all the other person's burdens, thus doing so much for him that we take away his freedom and his personal responsibility. When this happens we're likely to threaten him in a variety of ways, from taking away hope by the theft of the small goals of accomplishment that mark rehabilitation, to "protecting" him from family problems to the extent he feels isolated and no longer needed. It's best to work toward a balance, but usually if there must be a tilt, it's best to tilt toward helping him stretch just a bit more than he can comfortably do.

(2) Be available but not oppressive. Sometimes friends and relatives feel that they must be with the ill person all the time. But all of us need time alone...often the ill have a greater need for private time than the well. Being with a loved one all the time can be oppressive, as well as drain the strength of the relative or friend.

This means that loved ones should try to maintain as normal a life as possible, and be as natural as possible. And yet remain sensitive to the times when being there is important to the individual.

(3) Don't overload your own feelings. We've mentioned it before in this chapter. Often the emotional state of a spouse or close relative is drastically affected by the sickness of a loved one. There are sure to be times of depression, when the added stress seems more than one can bear. It's important then for the relative to get away, to relax, or to do something else which is a release from the tension at home.

(4) Stress the positive. As we saw in chapter six, even in the most serious situations there are aspects of hope. Those of us in helping relationships should constantly remind ourselves of the hope we have to offer to the ill. This will help us encourage him or her to a more positive attitude. It will also help us be positive about the situation.

(5) Be sensitive to the desires of the ill person. As much as possible let him plan his day. Relatives and close friends often make the mistake of planning for the person who is ill. Instead find out what foods he or she wants, what activities would be enjoyable, what goals that person may want to achieve.

(6) Don't back away from uncomfortable subjects. It's not unusual for an ill person to want to talk about his funeral or some other topic which may be uncomfortable for loved ones. If he wants to talk, then talk about it.

(7) Be sensitive to hidden needs. Often a person whose life is threatened will have a need to probe his own past and private experiences. Many of us carry bitterness or other burdens which we would like to see resolved. If it is at all comfortable for the ill person, be willing to explore past relationships where forgiveness and restitution may be required. We should not press in this area; if an individual does not want to share or probe the past, his desires must be respected. But at the same time reconciliation can be extremely meaningful when life is threatened.

Again in each of these areas we see a need to maintain respect for the ill person, and openness to his feelings and ideas and choices. Within the framework of love that is expressed as continuing respect for the individual, relatives and acquaintances can become what many life-threatened persons need most: friends.

Developing Sensitivity

> Personal projects for individuals or study groups to help develop sensitivity for ministry with the terminally ill.

1.   Write out your definition of being a friend.

2.   Try your hand at writing out imaginary dialogues, trying to show sensitive listening and responding. See the dialogues in the chapter for examples.

3.   The chapter stresses maintaining and showing respect for those with a life-threatening illness. Jot down as many ways as you can remember or think of that (a) medical personnel might show respect, and (b) family or friends might show respect. Then check your list against the specific suggestions found in this chapter.

Chapter 7, Notes

1. Anonymous, "Death in the First Person," in *Death: The Final Stage of Growth*, ed. Elisabeth Kübler-Ross (Englewood Cliffs, N.J.: Prentice-Hall, Inc., 1975), p. 25.

2. Randy Becton, *The Gift of Life* (Abilene, Tex.: Quality Publications, 1979), p. 71.

3. Sharon L. Roberts, *Behavioral Concepts and the Critically Ill Patient* (Englewood Cliffs, N.J.: Prentice-Hall, Inc., 1976), p. 156.

4. Elisabeth Kübler-Ross, *On Death and Dying* (New York: Macmillan Co., 1969), p. 118.

5. Ibid, p. 254.

6. Daniel C. DeArment, "Prayer and the Dying Patient, Intimacy Without Exposure," in *Death and Ministry: Pastoral Care of the Dying and the Bereaved*, eds. Bane, Kutscher, Naale, and Reeves (New York: Seabury, 1975), p. 53.

7. Dorothea Hays, "Anger: A Clinical Problem," *Some Clinical Approaches to Psychiatric Nursing* (New York: Macmillan, 1963), p. 112.

8. Roberts, *Behavioral Concepts*, p. 202.

Chapter 8

Models of Care

"I don't know what I'd have done without them," Betty told me. Then she went on to share her experiences of the last two years, and the emotional support she found participating in a group called Make Today Count.

When Betty's grandson was just two years old he was discovered to have leukemia. There was nothing anyone could do. They watched, helpless, as the child slowly died.

What made the situation even more tragic for Betty was that her daughter, who had married young, had chosen a husband who would not work and who often beat her. Rather than receiving support from the father, the two women were in constant fear of him. While her daughter worked, Betty took care of the grandson, suffering not only for him but also for her daughter.

Betty is not a Christian, and had no caring community of fellow believers to turn to. But she did find one source of help in a group of persons living with life-threatening illness. "I don't know what I'd have done without them," she told me.

And even now, a year after the child's death, Betty is in need of support. Her daughter left her husband for a time. But when he showed up again after a trip to California and demanded his wife return with him, she did. He still beats her. And Betty wishes the girl would leave him for good. But in the meantime she can do nothing but hope, and fear.

It's talking about her fears and listening as others share that make the monthly meetings of her Make Today Count group so important to Betty. "If I didn't have someone to talk to, someone who could understand, I know I'd never have made it."

It doesn't seem all that much. But the monthly encounters and the chats on the phone with people she meets seem to relieve the pressures and make it possible for Betty to go on. In fact, the relationships she's established mean so much to her that Betty coordinates one of the chapters of Make Today Count that meets in the Phoenix area.

Many have sensed the need of those whose lives are threatened or whose loved ones may have terminal illness. As the pattern of dying in America has changed (see pp. 10-11) there have been greater and greater needs for supportive relationships during times of extended illness. Some of the groups that have formed, and their approaches to caring for the terminally ill, suggest models of care that Christian individuals or teams from a local congregation can adapt as a pattern for their ministry. In this chapter we want to briefly sketch three of these models.

Make Today Count

P.O. Box 303, Burlington, Iowa 52601, (319) 753-6521 or 6522

Make Today Count was founded as a non-profit mutual support organization for persons with serious illness, their family members, and other interested persons. Today there are over two hundred chapters in many parts of the United States seeking to communicate the philosophy of the founder, Orville E. Kelly, who writes, "I do not consider myself dying of cancer, but living despite it. I do not look upon each day as another day closer to death, but as another day of life, to be appreciated and enjoyed." This thrust of hope and encouragement permeates the activities of the organization and the monthly newsletter it publishes.

The approach of Make Today Count is explained in the following material included in brochures published by the National Headquarters and the San Diego, California, chapter. That overview is quoted here.

What is Make Today Count? Make Today Count is a mutual support group composed of individuals who have encountered cancer in their lives, either personally or as a family member. They share their experience, strength, and hope in order to help each other live each day more meaningfully. In addition, persons with other life-threatening illnesses and interested community members are also invited.

What happens at a Make Today Count meeting? Make Today Count encourages honest discussion and the sharing of human concerns and emotions. Those who come discuss new resources and new ways of coping with problems. Sometimes the real help is simply being assured that another human being "knows" and understands the struggles and feelings expressed because he, too, has experienced them.

Chapter meetings are held twice monthly on an informal basis. Speakers are sometimes invited to share information of interest to the group. Examples of some local programs are: stress reduction techniques, values clarification, Social Security benefits, and Medi-Cal information.

Is Make Today Count a therapy group? Although an observable growth in mental health occurs and rising trust permits members to ventilate hurt, anger, and other emotions, Make Today Count is not a therapy group, nor are the chapter meetings referred to as therapy sessions. Appropriate referrals and professional therapy are encouraged when a need is indicated.

Does Make Today Count make recommendations regarding treatment? Make Today Count does not become involved in the discussion of medical treatment. Neither does Make Today Count provide nursing and homemaker services, nor material and financial assistance, although information on agencies that provide these latter services is available.

Does Make Today Count ask for any dues or fees? There are no dues or fees for Make Today Count membership. Each chapter is self-supporting through contributions and donations.

Is Make Today Count a religious organization? Make Today Count is not a religious organization nor is it allied with any religious denomination. However, spiritual and religious dimensions of one's personal experience may be shared.

Why is there a need for Make Today Count? Loneliness and fear often trouble cancer patients. Frequently they feel isolated by their own identity—"cancer patient." They often think of themselves as dying. Friends, relatives, and professional people tend to relate to them as dying persons. Many times life style changes, forced retirements, and limited social activities resulting from their cancer, contribute to their sense of loss and isolation.

Orville Kelly, a cancer patient since 1973, experienced these feelings and recognized the need to meet and talk openly with other cancer patients and their families. As a result, he founded Make Today Count in January, 1974 in Burlington, Iowa.

From Burlington, Iowa comes information on organizing a Make Today Count chapter.

Any community, regardless of its population, can support a Make Today Count chapter. Population, economic conditions, and social factors are not mandatory requirements. What is required is a group of dedicated people willing to volunteer their time and efforts to help others. This willingness to give, plus proper planning and hard work, can produce a permanent MTC chapter. The national office of Make Today Count is willing to provide the local group with all support possible in organizing a chapter, but the only certain factor of success is the determination of the local members to succeed in reaching their goal.

Organizational procedures. Just one determined individual can provide the impetus needed to get a Make Today Count chapter started. This has been demonstrated repeatedly. However, it is much easier if several individuals meet and combine their efforts to get the chapter organized.

Whether one or several persons take the initiative in organizing a chapter, a minimum number of members is needed to sustain an active Make Today Count group. This varies according to the size of the community. The support, the interest, and the advice of other local organizations are also helpful in forming a chapter, in recruiting members, and in launching successful programs. Among these are the medical professions, clergy, counseling services, local units of the American Cancer Society, social service departments of local hospitals, and the United Way cancer agencies.

Many of the initial difficulties of a newly-organized chapter can be avoided if the organizers remain aware of the three essential ingredients for an effective chapter.

(1) A clear purpose. It is difficult for a group to function if the membership hasn't agreed on the specific purpose for which the group was established. One goal of Make Today Count is for members to assist each other in learning how to lead a more fulfilling life; in short, how to "make today count." This can be achieved by the members drawing support from one another, by communicating different points of view, and by sharing personal experiences associated with life-threatening illness.

(2) Receiving new members. Make Today Count chapters which make it difficult for members to join—either by being very selective, or by "scaring off" prospective members, or by forming their own "cliques"—run the risk of growing very slowly or not at all. We believe that, within reason, Make Today Count chapter memberships should be open to all people seeking help which can be provided by the chapter. The composition of the chapter is very important. Make Today Count chapters are open to those who have a life-threatening illness, as well as relatives of such individuals, and also to doctors, nurses, and others involved in treating patients and counseling them. If one chapter grows too large, another group can be started.

(3) Maintaining group unity and providing a place for self-expression. One of the great inner strengths of Make Today Count has been that everyone feels free to express individual opinions without fear of reprisal or ridicule. This strength is reduced when a group begins to debate an issue. A first rule of successful groups, therefore, seems to be that everyone is entitled and encouraged to express his opinion. However, there are many ways of looking at an issue, and what may be "right" for one person may not be acceptable to another. Therefore, self-expression is encouraged but prolonged debate is not. If this "rule" can be kept in mind, heated arguments may be avoided. This does not mean everyone must agree, of course; but disagreements must be controlled. Encouraging people to talk about their personal feelings is important. However, members should have some assurance that what they discuss is confidential—and will be discussed only with other members of the group, unless previously agreed to be filmed or interviewed by members of the news media during a special, prearranged meeting.

In essence, Make Today Count encourages sharing for mutual support, and does not seek to control the direction of its individual chapters. For more information on this structure for caring, contact the organization's headquarters or read Orville Kelly's recent book, *Until Tomorrow Comes* (available from Make Today Count Book Department in Burlington for $9.95 plus $1 postage and handling).

Caring

P.O. Box 1315, Abilene, Texas 79604, (915) 698-4370

It was in 1973 when Randy Becton, then in his late 20s and working as a counselor with the Herald of Truth radio broadcast, learned that he had lymphatic cancer. His case seemed hopeless. Through three surgeries, dozens of tests, and two years of chemotherapy, the young husband with three children struggled with his disease. "My Christian faith," Randy says, "has been the anchor of my mental health, and my greatest source of comfort and hope. It helped me hang on and keep fighting. . . . It's made sense to me."

Finally his disease went into remission, a condition which is not a cure but in which the disease is inactive. It was then, from his personal experiences, that Randy wrote a short pamphlet to other Christians. *You're Not Alone* told what it's like to have cancer, and how to learn to lean on the Lord for strength. This was followed by another pamphlet and then, as letters and inquiries began to come in, by other written materials.

Since the 1977 pamphlets, Randy's concern for those who have a life-threatening illness has grown into an extensive ministry incorporated as Caring. The Caring organization is non-profit and volunteer, working with people in the Abilene area and, through written materials and audio tapes, to others across the country.

Unlike the other two programs described in this chapter, Caring is a distinctively Christian ministry. Presenting Christ and relationship with God as the anchor for meaningful hope in the face of a life-threatening illness is central to Randy's view of helping. A volunteer staff, presently numbering eighteen, shares this commitment to help individuals face-to-face and through literature.

Guiding principles. As the volunteer team has formed around Randy and his wife, Camilla, the team has stated several principles that guide its work with patients.

(1) We seek to understand the fears and uncertainties and unanswered questions which arise in the life of the patient and the family, and to share helpful information and encouragement to meet this need.

(2) We seek to tell people that they are not alone in fighting their serious illness; that a group of Christians care and are willing to provide various services to emotionally and spiritually support them in their battle.

(3) We seek to encourage people to look to God in their time of crisis and to find in Him the only permanent source of comfort, encouragement, and hope.

(4) We believe that people are important; we seek to stay in touch with them as they are undergoing treatment so that we can lend encouragement in whatever way possible.

(5) We try to empathize with those who live in an environment of pain and suffering and, while praying for them, to send them helpful tapes and printed materials which will be encouraging to them.

(6) We utilize the personal experiences of Randy, and others we know personally, to share possible solutions to the problems of depression, disappointment, aloneness, and other difficulties in the lives of patients and their families.

(7) We try to supply nurses, doctors, ministers, and other interested individuals with tools that will help them deal personally with cancer patients in their own locale. (Note: This has led to work with more than 100 ministers, 50 doctors, scores of nurses, and other health professionals.)

A brochure produced by Randy to explain Caring gives us a good overview of the kind of ministry which can grow out of Christian concern in a community. Here's how Randy explains the Caring ministry.

What it does. Randy formed the Caring ministry to offer support and comfort for cancer patients and their families.

Since he had been there and could identify with their emotions, he knew the need was enormous.

The Christian team which assists him in this ministry strives to be of practical help by writing letters or sending tapes and materials. The group meets twice a month for distribution of materials, new assignments, special training, and prayer. "Unlimited liability" is a phrase that describes the objective of the team. Offering themselves in love without limits is what Caring is all about.

Goals of the ministry. The Caring team's commitments to each person whom they seek to serve include:

(1) To assist those who are ill and their loved ones to find the strength from God for coping.

(2) To identify with the emotional needs and practical problems of those who are ill, sharing concrete suggestions which may be workable in the lives of those who are ill.

(3) To openly declare the necessity of making a commitment to God as the foundation for any successful system of coping with illness.

(4) To equip those who work with the ill with printed materials, tapes, and other resources so that their outreach may be meaningful and helpful.

What it is not. The ministry is *not* a clearing house for spreading news of recent medical advances or information concerning the results of certain medications and treatment procedures. Neither does the ministry engage in trying to steer people to a particular facility for treatment. This ministry concentrates instead on the task of supplying spiritual and emotional encouragement to each person in need.

Some questions and answers about the Caring cancer ministry.

Q. What is the source of the names of people who write the Caring ministry and want more information and materials?

A. There are several avenues:
(1) Letters from cancer patients
(2) Relatives and friends of cancer patients
(3) Referrals by doctors and nurses
(4) Publicity from articles in newspapers and religious periodicals, or radio and television programs.
(5) Churches

Q. What types of material are available?

A. (1) Booklets
(2) Paperback books
(3) Photocopied materials
(4) "Share Pieces"
(5) Poster size prayers
(6) Cassette tapes (also available in Spanish and Portuguese)
(7) Photographic posters
(A catalog of current materials is available.)

Q. How is the Caring ministry financed?

A. This is a personal ministry of Randy and Camilla Becton and is financed wholly by contributions from individuals who believe in the ministry as an effective outreach of Christian compassion.

Q. Who can belong to the Caring ministry?

A. There are eighteen committed Christians presently involved in this ministry. They represent varied backgrounds including the health care field. They are always open to more ways to reach out to hurting people.

Q. Is the Caring ministry affiliated with any church?

A. The ministry is totally non-denominational. Their efforts are used by congregations of Christians across the nation. The Highland Church in Abilene, Randy's home church, is especially helpful by providing bookkeeping services.

Q. What is the biblical motivation for this ministry?

A. No value can be placed on a person. Nothing in the world is as important. If people's needs are met, then we have fulfilled our mission. Jesus provides our model in John 9: (1) the man had a need—he was blind; (2) his need was met and the giver left the scene; and (3) he recognized that the giver had a personal relationship with God and wanted the same kind of relationship for himself, thereby opening the avenue to learn of the source of all comfort. We believe, therefore, that when a person's needs are met, it may open his eyes or clarify his vision of what can be accomplished with God. If we meet the needs of a cancer patient—if we can relieve some anxiety—help overcome some loneliness—help him to cope— then that's an opportunity for the works of God to become visible in a human life. That's the way God behaves, and He gives us an example through Jesus Christ.

In the material I've just referred to from one of Caring's brochures, there was a mention of printed and audio materials. One of the tapes, "Practical Suggestions for Visiting the Sick," is particularly helpful for those seeking to minister to the life-threatened. It is available from the Caring address given at the beginning of this section.

Hospice

National Hospice Organization, Suite 506, 301 Maple Avenue West, Vienna, Virginia 22180, (703) 938-4449

The modern hospice movement can be traced to England and to St. Christopher's Hospice, which opened in 1967. But the concept borrows from the Middle Ages and the religious communities that accepted pilgrims and cared for them until they were able to continue on their journey. St. Christopher's founders shared a distinctly Christian concern that motivated its establishment. In the words of the founder, St. Christopher's has since the beginning been "committed to the Christian faith 'in a spirit of freedom,' to giving service, 'in a spirit of quietness,' and above all, to the belief that 'love is the way through.' For many of those who work there this love is first of all expressed in the love of God, who has himself gone through death to resurrection and 'in whom all are made alive.'"[1]

Reports of St. Christopher's have stimulated a growing interest in hospices in the United States. In 1978 the AMA House of Delegates approved the hospice concept, that the terminally ill should be allowed to die at home or in surroundings more home-like and congenial than the unusual hospital setting.

In the British model there is "control of physical, sociological, psychological, and spiritual symptoms; coordinated home/inpatient care with a central hospice administration; inclusion of the family in the unit of care; provision of care by an interdisciplinary team including volunteers; structured staff support and communication systems; and acceptance of patients on the basis of need rather than ability to pay."[2] The goal of hospice treatment is not cure; it is care, with a goal of maintaining as desirable a quality of life as possible. The goal is to "allow a patient to die with dignity, freedom and self-respect," and at the same time to minister to the family as a group.

In the United States there are some 210 hospices operating or in the process of incorporating as of early 1980. The U.S. hospice programs are quite individualistic, with differing organizations providing different kinds of care, and incorporated with different goals. However, Dr. Kenneth P. Cohen outlines the common goals all share as:

- ease the physical discomfort of the terminal cancer patient by employing pharmaceutical and advanced clinical techniques for effective symptom control.

- ease the psychological discomfort of the terminal patient through programs allowing for active participation in scheduled activities or periods of peaceful withdrawal as determined by the patient.

- aid in maintaining the emotional equilibrium of the patient and the family as they go through the traumatic life experiences of progressive disease and ultimately the final separation of death.[3]

While the current U.S. hospice programs are individualistic, there is a coordinating organization and work being done by the medical profession as well as the government to find a most desirable pattern. Today most U.S. hospices focus on home care, with inpatient visits to hospitals. There are few residential hospices like St. Christopher's in the U.S. Cohen describes the elements of hospice services in his book.

"A hospice program is not just a program that purports to care for the terminally ill. It is a program for meeting a wide range of physical, psychological, social, and spiritual needs, a program of health care delivery consisting of ten clearly identifiable elements:

1. Service availability to home care patients and inpatients on a 24-hour-a-day, seven-day-a-week, on-call basis with emphasis on availability of medical and nursing skills.

2. Home care service in collaboration with inpatient families.

3. Knowledge and expertise in the control of symptoms (physical, psychological, social, and spiritual).

4. The provision of care by an interdisciplinary team.

5. Physician-directed services.

6. Central administration and coordination of services.

7. Use of volunteers as an integral part of the health care team.

8. Acceptance of the program based on health needs, not ability to pay.

9. Treatment of the patient and family together as a unit of care.

10. A bereavement follow-up service."[4]

Values of hospice. There is currently a surprisingly quick and wide acceptance of the hospice concept. There are a number of reasons for this acceptance. One motivating factor is the expectation that even inpatient hospice care may save patients and insurance carriers millions of dollars. The UCLA Cancer Center bulletin notes that "actual cost savings to families and insurance carriers can be considerable. Hospitalization can cost $180/day or more, whereas the Palliative Care Unit in Montreal reports that inpatient hospice care costs can be kept to about $100/day per patient. Outpatient home care services can be even less."[5]

Research in England suggests that hospice care tends to reduce depression, anxiety, and anger, although inpatient care was significantly more effective than outpatient in this regard. Yet both proved to be effective, and in fact "patients gave most praise to the outpatient system of care despite experiencing a little more anxiety and irritability at home."[6]

Probably the basic concern of the hospice approach is for the quality of life that remains for the patient. In a very real way the hospice focuses on care when treatment for possible cure has been abandoned. For most there is the assumption that the best place to die is at home. And in fact while a national study shows that most people do wish to die at home, only about 10 percent in the U.S. do so. Hospices have succeeded in reversing this and, in the program established by New Haven's Hospice, Inc., over 70 percent of the patients now die at home.[7]

It's clear that with the concentration on home care there may be additional strains placed on the family. But dealing with the family as a group is also part of New Haven's approach, with both professionals and trained volunteers ready to support the family and guide them as well.

In spite of the general enthusiasm for the hospice movement, a number of questions are being raised. The costs of
care in inpatient hospice facilities are generally only some 20
percent less than hospital care. Most who participate in the
outpatient programs do so only briefly, as they are terminally
ill when they enter. And, as Dr. John P. Callan asks of these
inpatient facilities, "do the patients and their relatives want to
have their loved ones transferred to these new places of little
hope?"[8]

A model for Christian care? Despite some of the trou-
bling questions and the relatively large amount of funding required, St. Christopher's and other hospices do provide a
model for the caring community to minister to the terminally
ill. And much help is available in establishing a hospice program in a local community. The National Hospice Organization and governmental agencies provide help and guidance,
and show how such a program can be established. Manuals,
and other forms of training help for volunteers, are also
available through the National Organization and individual
hospices. Because the approach is currently popular, the
medical community as well as government agencies are supportive. Groups with Christian motivations as well as individual believers desiring to serve as volunteers may find the
hospice a significant model for a ministry of care.

A simple brochure entitled "Support and Understanding
During the Last of Life's Passages..." produced by the San
Diego Hospice, summarized the ministry's approach and
what might be involved in establishing other hospices. Their
brochure states:

> *Hospice* is the name for a variety of organizations
> throughout the United States and in Europe that
> were formed to provide support, compassion, and
> practical assistance to the terminally ill, their
> families, and friends. The term Hospice was first
> used in medieval times to define a way station or

resting place for pilgrims traveling to and from the Holy Land.

Hospice believes that dying—a universal passage of life—evokes deep human needs. There is a natural need for understanding, sincere communication, and serenity on the part of the dying patient and all who share and care. The Hospice goal is to assist in the emergence of these positive and natural feelings so that one's last passage is as it should be—free from pain and stress, in an atmosphere of love and caring.

Hospice combines care with caring, establishing close communication with the dying patient, the patient's family and friends, and the attending physician to provide the most appropriate assistance in each individual case. To this end, Hospice services are flexible and carefully developed to meet the needs and wishes of each patient. In addition to providing emotional support, Hospice home care offers such services as:

- home visits—available seven days a week.
- practical assistance in personal and business affairs.
- nursing care—available in home or hospital.
- transportation and running of errands.
- spiritual and psychological support.

After the death of the patient, Hospice continues follow-up assistance and support to the family for a period of from six months to one year, enabling them to resolve the normal grief process.

Hospice services are available to any dying patient, regardless of age, race, religion, form of illness, or financial status. The only criteria are that the patient is aware the illness is terminal, the attending physician is in accord with Hospice services, and that the patient lives in the greater San Diego area.

The Hospice team in San Diego is comprised of an executive director, physician, registered nurse, social worker, chaplain, volunteer coordinator, medical records staff, clerical support, and certified home health aides. Augmenting this staff are more than fifty carefully screened volunteers who have completed thirty hours of intensive training prior to joining the Hospice team. In addition, Hospice may draw upon the professional talents of their Community Advisory Council which includes representatives from various social service agencies, community religious leaders, and national, state and local legislators.

Developing Sensitivity

Personal projects for individuals or study groups to help develop sensitivity for ministry with the terminally ill.

1. See if there is an organization in your community like one of the three referred to in this chapter. If so, visit its headquarters or one of its meetings. Afterward write out a brief evaluation of what you've seen, relating your observations as much as possible to the concepts explored in the rest of the book.

2. If you were to initiate or be a part of a group seeking to serve the life-threatened, which of the three approaches described in this chapter would you feel most comfortable with? Why? How many others whom you know might have an interest in forming a ministry team with you?

Chapter 8, Notes

1. Cicely Saunders, "Dying They Live: St. Christopher's Hospice," in *New Meanings of Death*, ed. Herman Feifel (New York: McGraw Hill, 1979), p. 174.

2. Marian Osterweis and Daphne Szmiskovicz Champagne, "The U.S. Hospice Movement: Issues in Development," *American Journal of Public Health* 69, no. 5 (1979): 492.

3. Kenneth P. Cohen, *Hospice* (Germantown, Md.: Aspen Systems Corporation, 1979), p. 4.

4. Ibid., p. 71.

5. *UCLA Cancer Center Bulletin* 5, no. 3, p. 16.

6. John Hinton, "Comparison of Places and Policies for Terminal Care," *The Lancet*, 6 January, 1979, p. 31.

7. Sandra M. Milolaitis, "Choosing the Circumstances of Death," *Forum* 2, no. 1 (1978): 21.

8. John P. Callan, "The Hospice Movement" (Editorial), *Journal of American Medical Association* 241, no. 6.

Chapter 9

A Basic Course in Caring

*I*nitially most of us feel uncomfortable in relationships
with the life-threatened. This is as true of professionals
who deal with the terminally ill in their work as it is with
volunteers, or members of a congregation who discover a
friend may be dying. It's important for all of us—including
members of families in which one member has a life-threatening illness—to have some kind of preparation. In this chapter
we want to examine training that might be provided, and to
integrate the concepts discussed in this book into a teaching/
learning process.

The training experiences are organized in fifteen two-
hour learning blocks. When possible it's good to provide the
training in a retreat format, or to hold a launching retreat followed by a series of weekly sessions.

The training design is distinctly within the framework of
Christian commitment and a biblical understanding of death
and dying. The training goal is to help build a more caring
Christian community, and to help individuals share Christ's
love with those living under the threat of a terminal illness.
Yet the training is adaptable for a number of different groups
and purposes. It might be used or adapted as an elective study

161

for members of a local congregation as general preparation for supportive relationships with friends or neighbors. Persons in a helping profession might use all or some of the training segments. Those called by God to form support groups (whether on the model of Make Today Count or Caring or Hospice) will find working through the training processes together important for them and for the future volunteers.

Training Philosophy

The training plan is based on several assumptions. We assume that both the attitudes and skills of the helping person must be dealt with. We also assume that Christian commitment provides a dimension of hope, and a basis for respect for the dying individual, which is vital in a truly supportive ministry. We also assume that the greatest need of an individual in life's final passage is for a significant personal relationship with God through Jesus Christ. The training plan, then, is designed to shape attitudes and to develop skills within the framework provided by the Christian faith's understanding of the significance of each human being.

If our goal is to shape attitudes and to sharpen skills, then we are immediately forced to special kinds of learning processes. Lectures do well in communicating facts. But lectures seldom affect attitudes, and do not provide practice for developing skills. To shape attitudes and gain skills, learning processes that feature interaction and sharing are required. So the training designs are highly interactive, with concepts introduced through reading and some in-class input, but with much of the group's time spent in talking through feelings and ideas.

To gain full benefit of the experience, either the training group should be small (not more than a dozen people) or a larger training group should be subdivided into groups of eight which will work together across the span of the whole training course.

The rest of this chapter is organized into fifteen separate training blocks. In case it is necessary to give less than the thirty hours of training recommended, a trainer may select from these blocks the ones he or she wishes to use, or may design substitute blocks. Each training block features a specific goal, gives background reading for the trainer, suggested reading or input for the trainees, and a plan for the learning experience. In general the blocks are organized in sequence, but here too the individual trainer may feel free to make adaptations.

Section I (blocks 1-4) deals with the individual's personal attitudes toward death and dying. Section II (blocks 5-9) deals with the reactions of the terminally ill individual and/or his family. Section III (blocks 10-15) focuses on responding to the life-threatened in a supportive and caring way.

Section I:
Personal Attitudes Toward Death and Dying

Block 1: *Numbered Days*

Goal: To examine our personal attitudes toward death in order to prepare for ministry with the life-threatened.

1. Form study groups of eight if the class is large. Have the group members share their names and why they elected to take this training.

2. Give the groups the following quote from the Psalms. Ask them to discuss what the psalmist is saying about death. What is his attitude toward death? What "wisdom" might an individual gain by numbering his or her days?

> The length of our days is seventy years —
>   or eighty, if we have the strength;
> yet their span is but trouble and sorrow,
>   for they quickly pass, and we fly away.
> Teach us to number our days aright,
>   that we may gain a heart of wisdom.
>   Psalm 90:10,12

3.   Give each individual the following questionnaire to complete. Do not explain it or how it will be used. You have permission to duplicate the quiz, and other similar activities for training purposes.

	Questionnaire	Agree	Disagree
a.	I have never thought of myself dying in a traffic or plane or some similar accident.	_____	_____
b.	I often read the obituary items in the paper.	_____	_____
c.	I see death as involving only a temporary separation from my loved ones.	_____	_____
d.	I think that medical science is likely to make discoveries that will extend my lifetime twenty or thirty years.	_____	_____
e.	I seldom think about death or dying.	_____	_____
f.	I think capital punishment is cruel and unusual punishment.	_____	_____
g.	It's always a tragedy when someone dies.	_____	_____
h.	I expect to face my own death calmly and peacefully.	_____	_____
i.	Exceptional medical means (drugs, support machines, etc.) should always be used to preserve no matter what a person's mental condition.	_____	_____
j.	I find it uncomfortable to think or talk about a person who has died.	_____	_____

k.   I am both fascinated and frightened
     to think about having a relationship
     with someone who may be terminally
     ill.   _____   _____

l.   If a person only has enough faith,
     God will always rescue him or her
     from the threat of death.   _____   _____

After each person has completed the questionnaire, have the group(s) discuss each question. What attitude toward death might an "agree" or a "disagree" answer to each item indicate? This discussion should take a group of eight at least a full hour. Please note that there are no "right" or "wrong" answers to this questionnaire. It is simply a way to help the learning group begin to deal with death and dying and to talk with others about this subject. It is also designed for one additional purpose, exposed in the next learning activity.

4.   After the hour discussion, ask each person to spend five minutes looking over the pattern of his or her answers to the questionnaire. On the basis of the answers and the preceding discussion, each is to see what insights he gains into his own attitudes toward death and dying.

     After five minutes for study, each group of eight should regather, and every member try to tell the others briefly what insight he has gained into the meaning death has for him or her.

5.   The trainer can conclude the first two-hour session by pointing out the importance of working through our own understandings and ideas about death, and learning to talk with others about this often taboo subject. This needs to be done before we seek ministry with the terminally ill or life-threatened. The trainer can also point out that the first part of this course focuses on building a personal attitude toward death that is both biblical and personally helpful.

| **Block 2:** *A Defeated Enemy* |

Goal: To examine biblical portraits of death and work
    together toward a "Christian perspective."

1.   Ask each person at the beginning of the session to write
    completions to the following open-ended statements.
    a.   To the Christian death is like...
    b.   A Christian should face death with...
    c.   The Bible pictures death as...
    d.   God's attitude toward death is...
    e.   When a Christian's loved one dies he...

When the open-ended questions have been completed, list
your group's responses on a chalkboard or flip chart. At this
stage it's not important to talk about the responses. Simply
list them for later interaction.

2.   In the group(s) of eight, discuss each of the following
    passages of Scripture. You may want to have the groups
work from a common version (the *New International Version*
and *Revised Standard Version* are good translations). From
the passages the group is to develop a set of 20 statements
that they agree are in harmony with "a biblical view of death
and dying." Passages to use are:

    Psalm 23; Psalm 73:23-26; Isaiah 38:10-14; Romans
    8:35-39; 1 Corinthians 15:50-54; 1 Thessalonians
    4:13-18; Hebrews 2:14-15.

3.   Share the statements each group has developed. Then
    compare them with the responses to the open-end state-
ments listed at the beginning of this session. Talk about any
differences between the sets of statements and sentence com-
pletions. Particularly explore to what extent the group and
the Scriptures view death as a "friend" and to what extent an
"enemy."

4.   Ask each person in the group to share an experience involving the death of someone close. How did he or she feel about the loss? How did the person approach death? As the assignment is given, stress listening sensitively to each other's experience, not to evaluate but to understand how each felt or responded.

5.   Conclude by having each person select one verse of Scripture (from the above list, or from another passage) which expresses his hopes or fears for his or her own death.

Block 3: *Fears*

Goal: To become sensitive to the fears associated with death and dying.

1.   Read aloud the following article, which appeared in the Phoenix, Arizona, *Republic* on Monday, February 25, 1980. After reading the article, discuss together: What fears does each member of the family seem to have? What feelings are associated with Mrs. Gardner's slow death?

Deathwatch

Family learns of life as Mom slowly dies

Life, says Sylvia Gardner, is like living with an ax hanging over your head and never knowing when it's going to fall.

Her ax is cancer. It was supposed to drop 13 months ago. It's still hanging, and Sylvia is still hanging on.

Mrs. Gardner is here with the help of the Community Home Health Care Agency, an arm of the Maricopa County Department of Health Services. She is enrolled in the Mayday program, which provides care for terminally ill patients in their homes. The program is set up to allow a patient to die with dignity and ensures that no extraordinary measures will be taken to prolong life.

A public-health nurse regularly visits Mrs. Gardner, as does a social worker, and together they attend to her physical and mental needs. For families like the Gardners, the Mayday program is a means of keeping the family together, at home. It also is designed to allow the family to share in the experience of dying.

For the Gardners, sharing cancer is a daily fight to remain calm and keep a positive outlook.

"I accept the fact that I have cancer," says Mrs. Gardner, who is 47. "I did not accept the fact that I was going to die when they told me I was going to die. I told the nurses that I was going home with my family to face this with them, together."

The Gardners live in a modest home in rural Tolleson. The family began facing the crisis together two years ago when Sylvia was diagnosed as having cancer of the uterus.

She lives quietly. Some days are better than others. There is constant pain, but she takes only vitamins. No more chemotherapy, no more experimental drugs. She says it's easier that way.

"Toward the end, it might get a little bit sloppy, a little heavy for my family," she said. "I don't want a bunch of needles and tubes stuck in me. For what? To watch my family die a little bit with me?"

When death comes, the program will take on a new course. The family will notify the emergency room at Maricopa County Hospital and ask for "Doctor Mayday." That will signal the hospital to dispatch a vehicle to the home to pick up the body. No frills, no flashing lights, no sirens.

Ray Gardner is a burly, nervous man who still seems to be angry at the cancer, at the doctors, at the ultimate unfairness that will claim his wife's life. She was dancing, and someone turned off the music. It is not a question of fairness.

At 43, he is a young man, but an industrial accident left him with a damaged back that won't allow him to work full time. He collects disability. He also cares for his wife and watches over their four children.

"Leave her?" He snorts at the question. "What choices have I got? When I was sick and hurt in a wheelchair, she stayed with me. But I get some nights that I want to get up and run. I get so lonely. I have to survive—I have four children."

The youngest, 9-year-old Bret, doesn't understand why his mother is sick all the time, even though the Gardners have tried patiently to explain the disease to him.

He draws pictures of his mother battling cancer. A stick-figure boy is shown punching a crayoned cancer cell. He frequently begs his mother to "give those old cancer cells to me, Mom, I can fight 'em for you; I can beat 'em up."

The eldest child, Barbara, is withdrawn and elusive at 17. She won't talk about the illness. She has the added burden of the household chores as well as riding herd over her younger brothers.

Mrs. Gardner spends her days in a bed or in a chair in the family room. She is thin and tired, and her voice reflects the minute-by-minute strain of her fight. She sees the situation as a learning experience for the children.

"It will help them," she says. "I feel positive about dying at home and letting them partake of it. When it happens, it's going to hit them hard.... But they can be in on it. I want my family to come closer together.

"They stand to lose their mother," she says. "They have to take over the house. They are going to do it as kids, not as adults. That's not easy."

The family dog, Apricot, a white poodle, curls up at Mrs. Gardner's feet. She smiles.

"I never did go through the angry stage," she says. "I never questioned and said, 'Why me?' I just accepted it as the will of God. I thank God I have had the time to get back into my church, to take a second look at my life and see what needed to be done."

Ray Gardner looks at his wife of 18 years who is reclining weakly on a chair. His eyes are misty.

"I'm mad about it, sure. I'm upset about it. But I can't do anything. You gotta sit and wait. That's what it's all about—being born and dying."

(Reprinted with permission of the *Arizona Republic*)

2.   Duplicate the list of common fears (below) which are included in Chapter 3. Ask each person to read the list and

pick out the three which he or she identifies with most closely, and put a check mark beside the three selected.

Fear of helplessness
Fear of being alone, deserted
Fear of pain and suffering
Fear of being a burden
Fear of humiliation
Fear of what will happen to projects
Fear of punishment
Fear of separation from loved ones
Fear of future for loved ones left behind
Fear of impairment, or being unable to care for self
Fear of the unknown
Fear of loss of emotional control

If the individual has other fears, they should be added to the list.

3.   In groups, again talk through each of the fears on the list (and any added by group members). Focus on these questions: What can a caring Christian community do to help deal with this fear? How might a friend offer support by word or action?

4.   The trainer should introduce the concept of "awareness states" (see chapter 1, pp. 16-17). Point out the problems associated with closed awareness, suspected awareness, and pretense. Only when there is open awareness—the situation in which the individual and those around him know the seriousness of the situation—can fears be brought into the open and dealt with. Caring for the life-threatened does not give us the right to force an individual to deal with the seriousness of his or her illness. Yet we do not want to make it more difficult to achieve an open awareness context. We need to be willing to talk about death and dying, and we need to accept fears as a natural and valid part of the experience.

5.   Conclude this session with two quotes from the psalms which illustrate the fact that the godly do experience fear

and other "negative" emotions—and that fears are an opportunity for each of us to grow in our capacity to trust. We must not reject or condemn others for their fears, any more than God does.

> My heart is in anguish within me;
>   the terrors of death assail me.
> Fear and trembling have beset me;
>   horror has overwhelmed me.
> I said, 'Oh, that I had the wings of a dove!
>   I would fly away and be at rest—
> I would flee far away
>   and stay in the desert;
> I would hurry to my place of shelter,
>   far from the tempest and storm.'
>   Psalm 55:4-8

> When I am afraid,
>   I will trust in you.
> In God, whose word I praise,
>   in God I trust; I will not be afraid.
> What can mortal man do to me?
>   Psalm 56:3,4

ASSIGNMENT: For those planning to continue the training sessions, the purchase of two books is recommended. Reading will be assigned from these two books for the rest of the session. The two books recommended are this text, and *On Death and Dying*, by Elisabeth Kübler-Ross. Read chapters 1 and 2 of this text.

Block 4: *We Count*

Goal: To help the participants see some of the differences
  that support from a caring community can make for the
  life-threatened.

1.   Reproduce, or read aloud, the quote from Randy Becton
      (pp. 20-21). Then work together as a whole group to
brainstorm (list ideas quickly without discussing their merits)
as many ways as possible in which a caring community can
provide support for an individual with a possible terminal illness, or for his family. Try to develop at least 40 or 50 items
on the list.

2.   Ask each person to rank personal concerns along a con-
      tinuum like the following: Each person is to imagine he
or she has a life-threatening illness, and to place only one
item on each segment of the continuum.

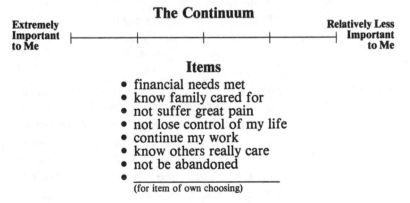

The Continuum

Extremely Important to Me |————————|————————|————————| Relatively Less Important to Me

Items
- financial needs met
- know family cared for
- not suffer great pain
- not lose control of my life
- continue my work
- know others really care
- not be abandoned
- _____

(for item of own choosing)

3.   Return to the groups of eight. Each is to show his con-
      tinuum, and share the ranking he or she gave each item,
with brief explanations why. Then, together, look at the list
from the first brainstorming activity. What actions might
believers take to provide support in the two most "important
to me" categories continuum?

4.   How does Christian faith help us deal with the areas ranked on the continuum above? The Christian has a distinctive view of who God is, and a personal relationship with God. Depending on the time available, let the groups of eight discuss each passage of Scripture listed below in relationship to the need items. Or divide into teams of two to four to cover half or one quarter of the passages.

The key questions to discuss are: What is God's commitment to us as His people? How can a personal relationship with God help the life-threatened?

Read Psalm 37:23-25; Matthew 6:25-34; Romans 8:38, 39; 1 Corinthians 10:13; Philippians 1:6; Hebrews 13:5b-6.

5.   The trainer can conclude this final session of Section I by reviewing several truths. God does care about the deep needs of the life-threatened. God acts through us, His people, to meet needs. Meeting needs means moving toward relationships with the life-threatened. There are many simple and yet important things that a caring community can do to provide support. There are, in personal relationship with God, great realities about who God is which provide the believer with a faith enabling him or her to face with confidence the fears that arise.

The trainer might conclude by reading the story of Ralph Neighbour's deacon (pp. 45-46, 51-52).

ASSIGNMENT: Read chapter 3 of this text. Master the "stages" of Kübler-Ross: that is, learn their names and be ready to write down a brief description of each if asked.

Section II:
Reactions of the Terminally Ill Individual

Block 5: *Denial*

Goal: To help the participants recognize and learn how to respond to denial behavior in a seriously ill person.

1.   The trainer should point out that the first section of the training (Blocks 1-4) familiarized the group with talking about death, and helped them become sensitive to common fears about and the Scripture's outlook on death and dying. The section now being begun focuses on reactions to life-threatening illnesses, and is designed to help group members recognize them and respond supportively. With this introduction the session itself can begin.

2.   One writer (see page 53) defines denial as "a general term used to cover any sort of behavior that allows a person to avoid facing reality, to evade a painful perception or to keep separate from it, or to escape confronting anything unpleasant." Share this definition, and ask the group members to discuss two questions:

   a.   Might denial ever be helpful to a life-threatened person?
   b.   Might denial ever be harmful?

3.   Following is a list of words and actions which may indicate denial. Duplicate the list, and have two persons from each group of eight study it for 10 minutes to prepare for acting out a "patient" role. Each is to plan how he might behave, and what he might say, if visited by a friend while trying to deal with an illness by denial.

a. Says he believes an error has been made by his doctor(s).
b. Explains disease symptoms as of another, less serious illness.
c. Says the doctor has promised quick restoration.
d. Never talks about death or dying; turns head away if dying is mentioned.
e. Talks constantly about plans for the future.
f. Openly says "I don't believe it."
g. Seeks treatment through non-medical remedy or God's healing.
h. Never asks questions about the disease or his symptoms.
i. Refuses treatment, expecting symptoms to disappear by themselves.
j. Does not recognize drastic changes in physical appearance.
k. Speaks of treatment or hospitalization as of very short duration.
l. Talks of illness as minor.
m. Knows what the illness is but professes to be sure he will recover.
n. Explains reasons why he or she can't die yet. (God wouldn't be so cruel; my children need me; etc.)
o. Does not seem to hear questions or comments on illness.[1]

4. While two in the group are studying the behaviors listed above, have the others study possible responses to a person's denial. Each is to decide which response he or she might make to a typical denial expression. Following are the patterns to be duplicated and distributed:

Patient Statement or Action   Response

a. "The doctor thinks it's cancer, but he's too young to really know."   a1. "I'm afraid no doctor would make a mistake about something as serious as that."

a2. "Don't you think you ought to consider whether the doctor might be right?

a3. "I understand treatment for cancer is becoming more and more effective."

b. "I think it's just a touch of flu, or maybe I've been working too hard."

b1. "I've never heard of flu hanging on as long as your illness.

b2. "I suppose that's possible, isn't it."

b3. "I guess the important thing is to take your medicine and rest."

c. "I don't believe it. This can't be."

c1. "I'm afraid it's true. And probably the sooner you face it the better."

c2. Silence.

c3. "I'm sure everyone feels that way for a time."

d. "I don't trust the doctors these days. So what I'm going to do is try a natural, all-grain diet."

d1. "Why don't you take your medication and forget about those quack fads."

d2. "How many doctors have examined you?"

d3. "Do you suppose the diet *and* the medication would make a good combination?"

e. "Next year, when we get these bills paid, I want to take a three-week travel vacation with my whole family."

e1. "Are you worried about getting the bills paid?"

e2. "That does sound relaxing."

e3. "Being with your family is important too, isn't it?"

5.   Have the two who studied the denial indications rejoin the others. Then ask the two to react to each response to the five statements in (4). Particularly they are to evaluate

each response from the point of view of the ill person on these criteria:

- • does this response help me openly share my thoughts and feelings?
- • do I feel this response is an attempt to force me to give up denial, or does it reinforce denial?
- • is this a *caring* response?
- • what other responses might be helpful?

6. The trainer will want to give a brief lecture on how to respond to denial. Principles to be observed include:
- • do not attempt to break through denial, but do not reinforce it.
- • try to let the person know that you care and are willing to talk about death or dying if and when the person is ready.
- • try to show that you do care.

7. Spend the rest of the time this session developing from list (3) possible statements or expressions indicating denial, and then together suggest a number of responses (as in list [4]). The responses should contain both good and poor examples, but should stress responses that the group feels fit the criteria listed in (5).

ASSIGNMENT: Read chapter III, "Denial and Isolation," from *On Death and Dying.*

Block 6: *Anger*

Goal: To help the participants recognize and learn how to respond to anger in the seriously ill person.

1. Duplicate for each person in the training group the *New International Version* of Psalm 73:1-14. In this psalm a

cause far less serious than that of a life-threatening illness (v. 3) has led one of God's people to bitterness, anger, and envy. Ask each to read through the psalm and underline words and phrases which show an anger-related emotion or its cause.

When completed, discuss in groups of eight. What emotions were discovered? What were their causes?

2.   How should we view anger? Is it an acceptable response?

Discuss this question openly, and then introduce into the discussion the quote from Kübler-Ross on page 57. Point out that of all reactions to the stress of life-threatening illness, this is the least socially acceptable. Yet it is a very understandable response. As human beings we, like the psalmist, are subject to feelings we have difficulty controlling. At times like these we do not need condemnation from others; we need a different kind of help entirely.

3.   Duplicate and distribute the rest of the psalm (73:15-28).

In your group of eight, try to trace the *change in feelings* of the psalmist. This is important, as you will want to establish that while such feelings as anger will exist at times, they need not *persist*. Specifically, explore and discuss these questions:
- What caused the change in the psalmist's outlook and feelings?
- What feelings replaced the feelings of anger?

4.   Together in your groups of eight evaluate the following responses to a person who expresses anger toward God or toward another person. Which are most likely to help him or her work through and beyond the anger?
- Stress the fact that anger is sin and insist he or she ask forgiveness.
- Strike back with an angry retort, so he or she can see what it's like to be hurt.
- Ignore the outburst.
- Apologize for whatever it is you've done, or agree with his or her attack on others.

- Try to express understanding of the anger though not agreement.

After the five options above have been discussed, move on to the next activity.

5.   Point out that condemnation—however communicated—is unlikely to help the individual with anger. He or she may repress the anger (cover it with self-control or no longer express it verbally) but that is unlikely to be helpful. Instead, showing acceptance of the person despite the anger, and encouraging him or her to talk about his feelings, is the most helpful approach.

What might accepting or encouraging responses be like? Here are a variety taken from a nurse/patient relationship training course.[2] Discuss each in the group.

Patient: "Get out of here! I didn't send for you—I have enough people pawing over me already!"

Nurse: "I'll be here when you want me."

Patient: "The doctors here don't know what they're doing! I can't get a straight answer out of any of them!"

Nurse: "Tell me what you want to know, and maybe I can get answers for you." (Sits down and makes it clear that she is ready to listen.)

Patient: "I told you I didn't want any visitors! Can't you leave me in peace!"

Nurse: "Call me when you want me—any time."

"I'll suggest that people call you before they come, so you can tell them if you feel like having visitors."

"I notice there are some visitors you don't object to. Can you tell me what makes them more comfortable to have around?"

Patient: "Jones will really be happy now! The- -- has been after my job for years!"

Nurse: "This man Jones—what is he like?"

Patient: (Throws the water pitcher on the floor.)

Nurse: "The pitcher isn't a bad thing to throw when you get mad. It's unbreakable."

"If you feel like getting it off your chest, I have time to listen."

Patient: (Turns impatiently to the wall when the nurse speaks to him.)

Nurse: "Please remember that I'm available to talk whenever you feel like it." (Makes a point of coming in regularly and sitting down for a few minutes, making it clear each time that she has time to talk—and listen—for a little while. Does this again and again, until she hits on a time when the patient is ready to talk.)

Patient: (Stares at the nurse belligerently when she asks a question.)

Nurse: "You look so angry." (Stated calmly)

Patient: (Pulls abruptly away when the nurse touches him.)

Nurse: "There are times when I hate having people touch me. When you're a patient, you probably get more of it than you want."

Patient: (Deliberately throws book on floor.)

Nurse: "You're very angry, aren't you?"

Patient: (Begins to put on his clothes and refuses to respond when the nurse protests.)

Nurse: "I know you're angry and hurt. Sit down and talk a while before you rush out."

6.   It's important to remember that anger may not be just a "psychological reaction" to the stress of life-threatening illness. It may also be caused by real needs that a helping person can meet. Review the true story of Jack (pp. 45-46, 51-52). His anger revealed real needs, and because those needs were expressed, members of one caring community did help. It's uncomfortable to be present when anger is expressed—and even more uncomfortable to be the target. But when we accept anger and encourage the individual to talk, we often discover practical ways to minister and to show God's love.

ASSIGNMENT: Read chapter IV, "Anger," from *On Death and Dying*.

Block 7: *Depression/Grief*

Goal: To help learn to recognize depression/grief and respond supportively to the seriously ill person.

1. Sometimes people label the grief or the depression experienced by those with life-threatening illnesses as "self-pity." A person with these feelings may be unable to express them because, like anger, they are not socially acceptable. In this session we first want to identify feelings associated with depression/grief, and to note actions or words which might express those feelings without being openly labeled.

Reproduce the chart on the next page which uses selected verses from Lamentations for each individual. Give 20 to 30 minutes to work alone or with one other person to complete the chart.

2. After individuals have completed the chart, share insights in groups of eight. Talk particularly about the fact that grief or depression are valid reactions to the reality of the potential loss from a life-threatening illness. If there is time, you might also introduce the following grief-related reactions.

Grieving Stages

shock (similar to denial)

disorganization (confusion, failure to follow through on regular tasks, loss of motivation)

volatile emotions (hysterics, anger, breaking things, locking self in room, beginning to drink, etc.)

guilt (blaming self, regrets over past failures, etc.)

loss and loneliness (intense feelings of abandoning or being abandoned)

(From Robert Kavanaugh, *Facing Death*, Los Angeles: Nash Publishing, 1973)

Biblical Expression	Feelings	Actions/Words that Might be Expected

Bitterly she weeps at night,
   tears are upon her cheeks.
Among all her lovers
   there is none to comfort her.
All her friends have betrayed her;
   they have become her enemies.
Lamentations 1:2		

The roads to Zion mourn,
   for no one comes to her
      appointed feasts.
All her gateways are desolate,
   her priests groan,
her maidens grieve,
   and she is in bitter anguish.
Lamentations 1:4		

"Look, O LORD, and consider,
   for I am despised."
"Is it nothing to you, all you who pass by?
   Look around and see.
Is any suffering like my suffering
   that was inflicted on me...?"
Lamentations 1:11b,12		

"This is why I weep
   and my eyes overflow with tears.
No one is near to comfort me.,
   no one to restore my spirit."
Lamentations 1:16		

I am the man who has seen affliction
   by the rod of his wrath.
He has driven me away and made me walk
   in darkness rather than light;
indeed, he has turned his hand against me
   again and again, all day long.
Lamentations 3:1-3		

Let him sit alone in silence,
   for the LORD has laid it on him.
Let him bury his face in the dust —
   there may yet be hope.
Let him offer his cheek to one who
   would strike him,
   and let him be filled with disgrace.
Lamentations 3:28-30		

Joy is gone from our hearts;
   our dancing has turned to mourning.
The crown has fallen from our head.
   Woe to us, for we have sinned!
Because of this our hearts are faint,
   because of these things our eyes grow dim
for Mount Zion, which lies desolate,
   with jackals prowling over it.
Lamentations 5:15-18		

Point out that many different actions can show this grief/ depression response, not just tears or moping.

3.   Distribute for discussion the "Ten Commandments" developed by Paul Johnson, included in this text on pp. 61-62. Ask each to think of one relationship he has now or has had with a seriously ill person, and to select the guideline which would have been most helpful in that situation. Use the ten to summarize some of the practical steps we can take in relationships with the terminally ill.

ASSIGNMENT: Review chapter 3 in this text, and chapters VI and VII from *On Death and Dying*.

Block 8: *Review*

Goal: To review normal responses of individuals to life-threatening illness.

At this stage of the training you will want to move to a new level of involvement: direct personal exposure. This can be accomplished in one of several ways.

1.   Invite a person with a possible terminal illness to visit your group and share.

2.   Invite someone from the community—a hospital chaplain, medical doctor, nurse—to meet with your group and to share, then remain for questions.

Each of these first two approaches has the advantage of allowing for personal interaction, an important step for your group toward building their own personal relationships with the life-threatened.

3.   Visit a nursing home and talk with the patients.

4.   Utilize one of the videotapes available from sources listed in the appendix.

5.   Use role play. Have volunteers take the role of a person with a life-threatening illness. Give each volunteer a brief description of his or her role. (For instance: The doctor has told you you have a serious illness but you are trying to keep this from your family.) Have other volunteers assume the role of a visitor to sit and talk with the individual, while observers watch. You may also find it helpful to tape-record the interviews. Then have the observers seek to identify the underlying problem or stage, comment on clues, and evaluate what the visitor did or did not say while relating to the "life-threatened" volunteer.

If you use a tape recorder, replay the tape and let both role players explain why each said what he or she did. Use the tape as a stimulus to the discussion and analysis.

ASSIGNMENT: Before the next meeting read chapter 4 in this text. Be prepared to define "social death" and suggest its possible impact on the patient and family.

Block 9: *Recognition*

Goal: To help the group discover how much they have learned about recognizing the feelings and needs of the seriously ill.

1.   Give each person a sheet of paper on which Psalm 88 has been printed. Each is to read through the psalm and identify common feelings or reactions of the life-threatened.

If you wish to give clues, have printed at the bottom of the page: social death, abandonment, guilt, fear, anger, despair, bargaining, depression.

After each is finished, read the psalm through together and identify the reactions.

2. "Social death" is illustrated in Psalm 88:4. Talk about this phenomenon and the tendency of those close to an ill person to "do too much," and thus strip away the prerogatives of self-determination. You might discuss the story of Jim Bevis's experience, reported at the beginning of chapter 4.

3. For the rest of the first hour of the session, read and talk over in groups of four, one or more of the transcripts of Dr. Johnson's interviews with the life-threatened, included in chapter 5. Again stress recognition of clues to the feelings and reactions that have been studied in this section of the training experience.

4. Use the second hour to help each individual gain some sense of what he has learned and how he has grown in the training experience. Ask each to write for five minutes about "Changes in my understanding and attitudes" that have taken place over the course of the training. Then in groups of eight have each person share what he or she has written with the others.

ASSIGNMENT: Study carefully chapter 6 of this text. Be prepared if asked to list the kinds of hope that do exist for a person with a life-threatening illness.

Section III:
Responding
to the
Life-Threatened

Block 10: *Hope*

Goal: To help trainees approach relationships with the life-
threatened with a positive attitude, and with awareness
of the hope that does exist for them.

1.   Hopelessness, as chapter 6 points out, comes when an individual feels that his future is fixed, when he has no significant goals, and when he has lost control of decisions that
affect his daily life. The chapter points out that there *is* hope,
even when a life-threatening illness has been diagnosed, or
when the illness seems terminal. One can never say with certainty when life will end. An individual need not lose control
of the patterns of his daily life.

More significant, however, is the basic question of what
makes any person's life meaningful and provides a valid
hope. So begin this session by evaluating with your group the
following statements.

    a.   Living for another twenty-five years would give my
life meaning and purpose in itself.

    b.   Finishing a project I am working on now would give
my life meaning and purpose.

    c.   Being able to do what I plan for the next year or so
would give my life meaning and purpose.

    d.   Having a good relationship with my loved ones and
contributing to others' lives would give my life
meaning and purpose.

    e.   Fulfilling God's plan for my life would give my life
meaning and purpose.

2.   After you have discussed each of the above, evaluate the
     statements in light of the following Scriptures: Matthew
6:31-34; Romans 13:8-10; I Thessalonians 4:11,12; I Timothy
6:11-16; James 5:13-16.

3.   Discuss: What *does* give meaning to a person's life? Does
     the fact that each of us will someday die — some sooner
     than others — really make a difference in meaning?

4.   Conclude the first hour by asking each person in the
     group to write his own obituary, seeking to express in it
some sense of what makes life meaningful to him — and what
would make his life meaningful. If there is time, these might
be shared in the groups of eight.

5.   For the second hour of the session place on a chalk-
     board, or duplicate and give to each participant, a copy
of the chart on p. 111. Spend the hour together seeking to fill
in each of the nine squares with meaningful kinds of hope to
hold out for those with a life-threatening illness. It will be
helpful for the trainer to reread the chapter and fill in his or
her own chart prior to the class session.
     NOTE: Communicating the gospel message of eternal
life will be covered more intensively in Block 13.

ASSIGNMENT: Reread chapter 6 of this text, and have
                    firmly in mind the kinds of hope that can
                    be encouraged in those with a life-threaten-
                    ing illness. It's possible that memorization
                    of the chart, or of key ideas from the chart,
                    should be encouraged to help fix the hope
                    outlook in each person's thinking. Also
                    study carefully chapter 7 of this text, with
                    special attention to the material on
                    listening.

Block 11: *Listening*

Goal: To develop skills for sensitive listening.

1.   Most of this two-hour period should be spent on the listening practice, involving both the reflective element and the sharing element illustrated in chapter 7. You might begin by making an audio tape of one or more of the dialogues reported in the chapter. Provide a copy of the dialogue to each individual. As the tape is played, ask each to follow along and to underline or otherwise mark responses which show sensitive listening. Then have the groups of eight talk about and compare their observations.

2.   Next divide into groups of four. Let two members of each group talk, one taking the role of a seriously ill person, the other the role of a friend. Simply carry on a conversation, with the friend practicing sensitive listening, especially the reflective and self-revealing elements. If it would be helpful, give each person a list (like the one below) with statements or actions designed to encourage the patient's expression of needs. These "starter" approaches, adapted from Epstein's *Nursing the Dying Patient*, will be helpful for each trainee to refer to later, when actually visiting a terminally ill person.

Encouraging Expressions of Needs
Showing readiness to listen
  1.   Sits quietly by bedside.
  2.   Asks, "Is there anything you'd like to talk about?"
  3.   Invites the patient to ask questions.
  4.   Asks, "How do you feel about being in the hospital?"
  5.   Asks, "How do you feel about your treatment?"
  6.   Says, "Tell me more about how you feel."
  7.   Asks, "Is there anything I can do for you?"
  8.   Waits several seconds for the patient to respond when asked a question.

9. Nods, showing acceptance of what the patient says.
10. Reveals, "Yes, something like that happened to me."
11. Responds by building on what the patient says.
12. Talks about patient's family, friends, work, etc.
13. Expresses sadness to match patient's sadness.
14. , Says, "I'm so sorry you. . . ."
15. Expresses anger to match patient's anger.
16. Says, "I'm sorry I can't change things for you."
17. Cries when patient cries.

3. After all individuals in the groups of four have had the opportunity to play each role, and to have their listening techniques critiqued by the two observers, have each person *write out* one or two imaginary dialogues between a patient and friend. The dialogues should illustrate good listening, and the expression of feelings and needs which can flow from it.

After each has spent some 10 minutes or so writing out dialogues, these should then be read in the groups of four. Others may make comments on the dialogue, pointing out good examples of sensitive listening, and possible suggested changes or additions.

ASSIGNMENT: Encourage each person to practice his listening skills with at least two different individuals before the next session. He may use the skills with family members or with friends. Afterward, write out the conversations as accurately as possible, and bring them to the next training sessions. Also, reread chapter 7, with special concentration on the role of prayer in a helping relationship. And bring Bibles to the next session.

Block 12: *Prayer and Scripture*

Goal: To help the trainees gain understanding of how to share prayer and Scripture with the life-threatened.

1. Begin by asking each person to take about 15 minutes with his or her Bible, and find 5 to 10 verses which might be meaningful to the life-threatened.

2. After the verses have been located, suggest these criteria for Scriptures to use:
   1. Be relevant to the needs of the life-threatened
   2. Emphasize personal relationship with God
   3. Focus on who God is and His love for us

You may also want to introduce two passages, such as Psalm 23 or Hebrews 13:5b, 6 as examples. Talk together about how each of these fulfills the three criteria above.

3. Select one or two of the interviews from chapter 5 to read aloud. Then ask each person to select one of the passages he selected which might be meaningful to that individual. As each shares the Scripture he selected, have him explain *why* that verse or passage would be appropriate.

4. Finally, conclude this section on Scripture by developing a common list of appropriate passages. Share all the verses selected in (1). Suggest the group memorize a number of the passages so they can be naturally shared with others.

5. Both Scripture and prayer will normally be introduced as part of the listening and sharing that takes place between a friend and the life-threatened. "Preaching," or seeking to convince the other of a doctrine or truth, seldom is appropriate. Instead, the great realities of faith that bring hope and comfort will come as a natural part of the conversation. The focus will be on the individual's needs, and on God, who

loves him and is able to meet those needs. Prayers will typically be brief, and meet the same three criteria for choice of Scriptures.

1.   Be relevant to the needs of the life-threatened.
2.   Emphasize personal relationship with God
3.   Focus on who God is, and on His love for us.

The trainer will want to restate these principles as the area of prayer is introduced.

6.   At this point one of two approaches might be taken.
Either go back to the cases used in (3) above, and ask each person to write out brief prayers which he or she might pray with those individuals. Share the written prayers in the groups of eight. Or go back to role play, and have one person take the role of the individual in the case study. Another can be the visiting friend, while others observe. The goal is for the person playing the visitor to practice sensitive listening, and when appropriate to introduce Scripture or prayer.

ASSIGNMENT: Have each reread pp. 117-20 of chapter 6, which tell of the conversion of Senator Powell.

Block 13: *Sharing Christ*

Goal: To learn to more effectively share Christ and the Gospel with the life-threatened.

1.   Begin by having the trainees share in groups of eight how they first heard about Jesus, and the factors that led to them becoming Christians.

2.   Play a tape recording of someone reading Paul Johnson's story of the state senator (from chapter 6).

Ask the group to write down as they listen any principles they observe that seem important to them. Then discuss their observations.

Afterward restate the principles suggested in the text:
a. Listen to show respect before trying to witness.
b. Do not impose; share the Gospel as an affirmation of your personal faith.
c. Stress personal benefits and present experience.
d. Focus on personal relationship with Jesus, not church affiliation or subsidiary doctrines.

3. Distribute the booklets *Who Can I Turn To?* by Paul Johnson, to each class member. These are designed to address the questions of those who have been told they have a life-threatening illness. Talk through each page, noting *what needs* are dealt with, *what Scriptures* are used, and *how the Gospel is presented.*

4. Discuss the relationship of *acting to meet needs* (as in the case of Jack, chapter 3) with sharing the Gospel. Discuss too the idea of "winning a hearing." What gives others confidence in your love so that they realize when you share Christ there are no ulterior motives?

ASSIGNMENT: Read chapter 9 of this text for models of care.

Block 14: *Models for Care*

Goal: To help the group see ways that others have banded together to meet the needs of the life-threatened.

This session should expose your group in as significant a way as possible to existing organizations that minister to the life-threatened. Chapter 8 discusses three different groups that have been organized to provide support. It's likely that one of these organizations has a chapter within driving range. It's recommended that this session be a "field trip," and that you visit such an organization or one of its meetings.

A phone call to the numbers provided in the text should help locate chapters in your area. Or ask your doctor or local medical society for a source.

If there is no such group in your area, you might check with the local university to see if they offer courses on thanatology. A teacher of that course may be a resource person to invite to your session.

A final option if none of the others are available might involve rental of a speaker-phone, and phone calls (arranged in advance) to those involved in various ministries. With a speaker-phone your group members can ask questions as well as listen.

Whichever approach you take, talk ahead of time about what information you would like to have, and what questions should be asked.

Block 15: *Hearing God's Voice*

Goal: To help individuals and the group sense God's leading for them in this area of ministry.

This session is not designed to force or to manipulate. It *is* designed to confront the question of God's intention for your group, and for its individuals.

1.   Have each person take 10 minutes to write out his or her "vision." Each should write on the subject, "How I see God using this training in the next five years."

It may be that individuals will think in terms of personal opportunities to share. But some may think in terms of an organized effort: something on the order of a Make Today Count chapter or a hospice.

2.   Then have each person share what he or she has written with the others.

3.   This should lead into a general discussion of what vision God may have for a ministry to the terminally ill in your community. There should be no attempt to force shaping of an agency or program. But if God is calling some to an organized concern, the sharing will help them sense that call and begin to build a ministering team. Those who want only to be ready to minister to friends or neighbors without further organization should also be affirmed.

Chapter 9, Notes
_____

    1. Adapted from Charlotte Epstein, *Nursing the Dying Patient* (Reston, Va.: Reston Publishing Co., 1975), p. 22.
    2. Epstein, *Nursing*, pp. 41-46.

Chapter 10

Resource Review

*T*here are multitudes of published books and articles that relate to ministry to the terminally ill. Some 800 books are currently in print in English. These range from technical medical studies and textbooks, and psychological and sociological studies to more popular books, which explore everything from funerals to the currently popular "return from the dead" experiences that have been medically named the "Lazarus Syndrome."

In addition there are a number of books which tell personal stories. These are often beautifully and sensitively written, and reflect both Christian perspectives and contemporary humanism.

It would be impossible, and hardly helpful, to review all of these publications. Instead we have chosen to point you toward books that will be supplementary, within the framework of the purpose of this text.

This book was written from a distinctive perspective, which does make it different from other publications. Our goal has been to distill the basic information needed by believers to understand the strains of terminal illness, and to suggest ways that Christians—whether ministers, medical professionals, or simply members of a local congregation — can minister to the life-threatened. We believe there is a significant ministry that can be performed only by a caring Christian community. So our desire has been to show, with illustrations and information, *what* believers can do. And to show with principles and a training plan, *how* we can equip to reach out and minister.

These purposes have shaped our selection of resources. We have not tried to list or annotate *all* available materials. Instead we have tried to carefully select resources which might supplement this text and be useful in helping prepare believers for an active caring ministry.

Many significant resources are not listed here. Our goal, again, has not been to be exhaustive, but to guide to resources which would be significant additions to a church, medical, or personal library as supplementary reading to the training process outlined in chapter 9.

Books

Professional books. Books in this category go in depth into issues related to terminal illness. They tend to be academic in character. At the same time, they are significant because they deal in a substantial and significant way with critical concerns. For instance, Roberts's book has excellent chapters on hopelessness which, while her focus is the nurse in a critical care unit, have broad application for all relating to the life-threatened. Books in this category will be helpful primarily to the professional, or to the person leading training, who wants to enrich his own background.

1. Charles Garfield, *Psychosocial Care of the Dying Patient*, McGraw-Hill Book Co., 1978.
2. Charles E. Hollingsworth and Robert O. Pasnau, *The Family in Mourning: A Guide for Health Professionals*, Grune & Stratton, 1977.
3. Sharon L. Roberts, *Behavioral Concepts and the Critically Ill Patient*, Prentice-Hall, 1976.
4. Avery Wiseman, *Coping with Cancer*, McGraw-Hill Book Co.

Popular books (secular). Books in this category are in paperback form, and inexpensive enough to be used as collateral readings for those in a training course, or with a general interest in this area. There are many such books available, but the ones the authors believe will be most helpful to the general reader are:

1. Elisabeth Kübler-Ross, *On Death and Dying*, Macmillan, 1969.
2. Elisabeth Kübler-Ross, *Questions and Answers on Death and Dying*, Macmillan, 1974.
3. Michael A. Simpson, *The Facts of Death*, Prentice-Hall, 1979.

Simpson has an excellent annotated bibliography. However, his appendix, entitled "Resources," is already seriously out of date, and many of the organizations referred to no longer are in existence.

Special areas. There are within the general field of thanatology several highly specialized areas. Two have been selected for special reference here, because they are areas which the Christian community is likely to confront.

(1) Hospice. Many articles are currently being published in medical and public health related journals. However, rather than trying to trace them down, the reader will find all the information needed in three locations. The first source is the National Hospice Organization, Suite 506, 301 Maple Avenue West, Vienna, Virginia 22180, phone (703) 938-4449. This organization responds quickly to requests for information relating to the hospice movement, and has many helpful working papers and publications. The other two sources are new books.

1. Kenneth P. Cohen, *Hospice: Prescription for Terminal Care*, Aspen Publications, 1979.
2. Michael P. Hamilton and Helen F. Reid, editors, *A Hospice Handbook*, Eerdmans, 1980.

(2) Children. A number of sources explore experiences with children about death. These range from studies of dying children (Bluebond-Langner) to guides for answering parents' and children's questions. These books are most helpful.

1. Myra Bluebond-Langner, *The Private Worlds of Dying Children*, Princeton University Press, 1978.
2. Earl Grollman, *Talking about Death: A Dialogue Between Parent and Child*, Beacon Press, 1976.
3. Anna Wolf, *Helping Your Child to Understand Death*, Child Study Press, 1973.

Christian books. There is an ever-increasing number of books produced by Christian publishers in this area. These range from first-person stories, to a few new books which do more to explore the whole area from a Christian perspective. At the risk of offending those whose excellent books were left out, the authors believe the following would make good collateral reading, and could be useful in a church or other Christian resource library.

General books. These books give some insight into the relationship of the Christian community to death and dying, and are helpful for motivating involvement of Christians with the life-threatened.
1. Randy Becton, *The Gift of Life*, Quality Publications, 1979.
   This paperback tells Randy's personal story. Its particular value is the insight given into the support that can be provided by a caring Christian community.
2. Ruth Kopp, *Terminal Illness*, Zondervan Publishing House, 1980.
   This book by a professional counselor is sensitive and positive, and will build both understanding of terminal illness and values of Christian faith.
3. J. Kerby Anderson, *Life, Death and Beyond*, Zondervan Publishing House, 1980.
   This book is included only because it deals with several contemporary fads such as out-of-body experiences, paranormal experiences, and reports of after-life experiences by those who have supposedly "died" clinically. It does include also a good bibliography, including several sources for audio tapes.

Enriching reading. These books make enriching and thoughtful reading.

1. Joe Bayly, *The View from a Hearse*, D.C. Cook, 1973.
   A brief paperback in which Bayly shares from his own family's experience of the death of several children.
2. C.S. Lewis, *A Grief Observed*, Seabury Press, 1961.
   Lewis' experience after the death of his wife.

Videotapes and Films

One possibility for special input in your training sessions (see chapter 9) is found in videotapes or films. Typically educational film libraries (contact your local college for catalogs) will have a number of films on this general subject. Read their descriptions and choose those which seem best suited to your specific purposes. Because new films are being added, it's best to check directly with current catalogs rather than to rely on lists found in books, which will be incomplete at best.

However, today another source of visual materials exists in the videotape materials being produced by many teaching hospitals. For instance, the University of Texas System Cancer Center, in Houston, Texas, lists scores of motion pictures and videotapes covering every aspect of that disease. Four from their listing illustrate the kinds of resources which can be particularly useful in training.

899-1-78 Pastoral Care of the Cancer Patient
997-1-78 Clinical Oncology Grand Rounds: "Psychological Aspects of Cancer"
 87-1-74 Fear, Hope and Fulfillment in the Care of the Cancer Patient
197-1-75 Spiritual Needs of the Cancer Patient

This last videotape gives an excellent and sensitive overview.

It's best to look to cancer centers in your own state or a nearby metropolitan area for films or videotapes. However, if there is no local center, the videotapes above can be ordered, and a catalog obtained, from:

Department of Medical Communication
The University of Texas System Cancer Center
M.D. Anderson Hospital and Tumor Institute
Texas Medical Center
Houston, Texas 77030
713/792-6746

Tools

Most books written on death and dying are directed to those who may be in a helping profession or other relationship with the life-threatened. Few are suitable for the person who has been told he has a serious illness, or who is experiencing increasing difficulty from a probable terminal disease.

One problem with many of the booklets that are directed to the life-threatened is that they either do not focus on the specific concerns and fears of the life-threatened, or they are too long to be read comfortably. Normally there is sufficient shock and denial when a person hears his diagnosis that he is unable or unwilling to read longer books that demand some level of concentration, and whose goal is to "explain" rather than to touch the deeper areas of concern immediately and provide support.

To meet the need for a brief, direct, and supportive booklet which an individual might give to a person with a life-threatening illness, the authors of this text have produced *Who Can I Turn To?*, which shares from Dr. Paul Johnson's own bout with cancer. In a very simple and personal way, Paul speaks of his experiences and feelings, constantly offering the very real hopes that exist for the life-threatened, and sharing those Scriptures which have deep personal meaning for those who walk in the valley of the shadow of death. Great care has been made to build into the booklet the principles of relationship and communication taught in this text.

As a tool, then, the booklet is designed to be used by ministers, chaplains, doctors and nurses, and friends who make contact with the life-threatened. The booklets are available at your local bookstore or can be ordered from Multnomah Press, Portland, Oregon 97266. *Who Can I Turn To?* will not only minister directly to the life-threatened, but will also provide a door opener for talk and sharing.

Scripture Index

Subject Index

Abandonment
ministry to, 62, 135
occurrence of, in Psalm 88, 79
Acceptance
as stage of dying process,
59-60
in response to patient's
feelings, 32, 33, 59, 127,
131, 179
Adam and Eve, 30
Advocate, 66, 69
Affirmation, 36
Affirmation of Life, 41 fig.
Anger
as stage of dying process, 56
examples of, 56
occurrence of
in family, 70
in Psalm 73, 57-58, 178
in Psalm 88, 79
responses to, 56, 136, 178-180
Ansel, Ruth A., 69
*Archiv für Psychiatrie und
Nervenkrankheiten,* 49
Attention, 125
Availability
importance of, 62, 69
maintaining balance in, 140
Awareness states, 16-18, 170

Bargaining
as stage of dying process, 58
occurrence of
in family, 71
in Psalm 88, 79
Becton, Randy, 20, 124, 149
*Behavioral Concepts and the
Critically Ill Patient,* 104

Bevis, Jim, 65
"Beyond death" experiences, 42
Bill of Rights, Hospital
Patient's, 19 fig., 20
Biofeedback, 109

Callan, John P., 157
Cancer
attempted treatments for, 109
examples of, 7, 14, 88, 123,
124
blood, 87
breast, 85
colon, 45, 91
leukemia, 143
liver, 94, 107
lymphatic system, 114, 149
neck, 118
pancreas, 113
spine, 86
uterus, 168
Caring community
attitudes for ministry, 21-22,
32-43, 49, 60-62, 107
barriers to ministry, 15, 21,
77-81, 123
basis for ministry, 10-13, 18
cautions for ministry, 39, 62
examples of ministry, 7-8,
20-21, 73, 80-81
forms of ministry, 36-37,
52, 172-173
model for ministry, 43
results of ministry, 52, 80
scope of ministry
to the terminally ill, 12, 52,
112

205